6v

S. 17

THE BANK FOR
INTERNATIONAL SETTLEMENTS

MACMILLAN AND CO., Limited
LONDON · BOMBAY · CALCUTTA · MADRAS
MELBOURNE

THE MACMILLAN COMPANY
NEW YORK · BOSTON · CHICAGO
DALLAS · ATLANTA · SAN FRANCISCO

THE MACMILLAN COMPANY
OF CANADA, LIMITED
TORONTO

THE BANK FOR INTERNATIONAL SETTLEMENTS

BY

PAUL EINZIG

D.Sc. Pol. & Econ. (Paris)

FOREIGN EDITOR OF "THE FINANCIAL NEWS" AND OF "THE BANKER"
EUROPEAN CORRESPONDENT OF "THE BANKERS' MAGAZINE", NEW YORK
AUTHOR OF "INTERNATIONAL GOLD MOVEMENTS", ETC.

MACMILLAN AND CO., LIMITED
ST. MARTIN'S STREET, LONDON

1930

PRINTED IN GREAT BRITAIN
BY R. & R. CLARK, LIMITED, EDINBURGH

PREFACE

ALTHOUGH the plan of the Bank for International Settlements was a matter of lively discussion during the last few months, its critics have confined themselves almost completely to its general aspects. This is only natural. Technicalities are out of the range of theoretical economists, and the scheme, at its present stage, is too vague to provoke bankers to criticise its details. The author, who occupies an intermediate stage between academic economists and practical specialists, attempts in this book to fill the gap, and aims at providing material for the discussion of neglected technical aspects of the proposed institution. In doing so, he has to break entirely new ground, which explains, and perhaps excuses, the shortcoming of his book. If the attempt has no other result than to stimulate the discussion of the practical details— upon which the scheme will, after all, stand or fall—he will feel that his efforts were not altogether wasted.

The book gives comparatively little attention to the reparations aspect of the scheme, as in that respect the Young Plan is for the most part self-explanatory. Its chief concern is with the problems connected with the international banking activities of the Bank for International Settlements, such as the proposed gold clearing

v

system, the problem of a "world bank rate", the possibility of credit inflation, the danger of political interference with the management of the Bank, &c. For the convenience of readers, the text of the preliminary announcement of the scheme, the statutes of the Bank, and those portions of the Young Plan which touch the Bank are reproduced in the Appendices.

It will be seen that the author, though in favour of the scheme as a whole, nevertheless shares the fears of those who consider the Bank a potential source of international credit inflation. It is of great importance that public opinion should realise the extent of the danger of political influences upon the Bank. While in the case of the League of Nations—with which the Bank is frequently compared—this factor could, at its worst, merely lessen the beneficial effects of the activities of that institution, in the case of the Bank it could wreck the scheme altogether, and might cause incalculable harm to the credit system of the world.

Part of Chapter X. was published in the September 1929 issue of *The Economic Journal*, while parts of various chapters appeared anonymously in the daily "Lombard Street" column of *The Financial News*, and in an editorial article published in the December 1929 issue of *The Banker*. The author wishes to thank the editors of these publications for their permission to reproduce them here. He is also indebted to those bankers with whom he has discussed the problems dealt with in this book; these exchanges of views helped him to a very great extent to make up his mind on several controversial points. His thanks are especially due to Mr. C. I. Carr Bosanquet, for his valuable suggestions and candid criticism, which have been of great assistance to the author. He is equally indebted to one of the participants of the Baden-Baden Conference for having revised the book, while in proof, with critical eyes.

P. E.

20 BISHOPSGATE, E.C.2,
    December 1929.

PREFACE TO THE SECOND EDITION

SINCE this book was written the scheme of the Bank for International Settlements has been definitely adopted by all the parties concerned, and arrangements have been made for the new institution to begin business at an early date. The Statutes elaborated at Baden-Baden were adopted at The Hague practically without alteration, so that, when revising the book for this second edition, there has been no need to make any changes in the text on that account. On the other hand, in response to constructive criticism, and in view of the development of the scheme, the author has made some minor alterations in various chapters and has added another chapter. The Appendices have also been completed by the addition of the Charter, Trust Agreement and all clauses of The Hague Agreement of January 20, 1930, and its annexes which referred to the Bank.

The author's main thesis, that the new system carries the possibility of inflationary credit expansion—a contingency which necessitates most conservative management—was contested by various critics. Nothing that has been said, however, has altered his views, as expressed in Chapter VIII., which has been reprinted here

practically without modification. On the other hand,
the author considered it necessary to remedy an important shortcoming of the first edition; he owes a debt
of gratitude to Sir Josiah Stamp for having drawn his
attention to it in his review of the book published in the
columns of *The Financial News*. As Sir Josiah rightly
pointed out, the book did not lay sufficient stress upon
the importance of the Bank's task in arresting a decline in the world level of prices. This criticism induced
the author to conquer his dislike for metaphysics and
to devote an additional chapter to the fascinating but
elusive subject of "The Bank and World Prices". This
chapter and the preceding chapter on the "Credit Resources of the Bank" are complementary to each other.
Both deal with the Bank's power to bring about an extension of international credit resources; while Chapter
VIII. gives warning against the abuse of that power for
inflationary purposes, the new Chapter IX. indicates
the scope for its legitimate and desirable use, *i.e.*, to
prevent a decline of the international price level.

The new chapter, too, contains a warning that even
the legitimate use of the Bank's exceptional resources
for fighting deflation is not without dangerous possibilities. An institution which sets itself the task of
regulating world prices may easily become a hunting-
ground for doctrinaires. The worship of index numbers—
which is as fashionable among the economic experts of
our generation as was the cult of the "economic man"
among nineteenth-century economists—if practised
without due discrimination as to the causes of the

changes in the price level, may easily lead to the adoption of an unsound policy in the matter of price regulation.

By the time the present edition reaches the reader the Bank will probably be in operation. The Board and Management will be faced with a series of difficult initial problems, and the way in which they solve them will powerfully influence its future course. It is, therefore, of particular importance that informed opinion should follow closely its activities during the early period, and should be able to criticise if and when it becomes necessary, before any initial errors develop into integral parts of the system. Hence the necessity of greater knowledge on the part of the general public of the organisation, potentialities, means and ends, resources and shortcomings of the Bank for International Settlements.

P. E.

20 BISHOPSGATE, E.C.2,
    March 1930,

CONTENTS

xiii

CHAPTER I

In March 1929, almost to a day two hundred years after the death of John Law, and within a few hundred yards of the scene of his activities, the scheme of a bold experiment, worthy of the genius of that financier, was elaborated in Paris by a body of distinguished experts. It is pregnant with immense possibilities, but also with great dangers. It is as ambitious and as perilous as was John Law's scheme for a bank of issue in the less advanced conditions of eighteenth-century France.

The world was taken by surprise when it was announced that the Committee of Experts on Reparations had decided to propose the establishment of an International Bank. The novelty and boldness of the idea appeared fascinating to some people, bewildering to others. Although many months have passed since the announcement was made, and fuller details of the scheme have been published in the meantime, public opinion has found it difficult to crystallise into any definite attitude upon the merits or demerits of the proposed plan. Expert opinion is fairly evenly divided between adherents and opponents of the scheme, while the predominant feeling among the general public is that of curiosity mingled with distrust—that instinctive distrust of the average man towards any creation of genius which threatens to interfere with the routine of the Universe.

1

Ever since the war, it has been a commonplace all over the world that the remedy of our present evils will have to come through natural development and not as a result of any brilliant ideas. Any suggestion of miraculous remedies was dismissed with disdain by economists and by those responsible for official monetary policies. Without warning, these same ultra-conservative quarters produced now a scheme full of imagination and innovation. It is not surprising that the uninitiated public, which has always been told to beware of radical remedies, is confused and is at a loss to decide what attitude to take up.

If the scheme of the International Bank were nothing more than the product of a few imaginative brains, there would be, no doubt, good reason to receive it with distrust. The fact is, however, that the proposal made by the Young Committee is the logical outcome of the evolution of post-war financial history. It is not a mere accident that the creation of the Bank was proposed in 1929 and not in 1913, or 1923, or 1933. Anybody bold enough to make such a suggestion before the war would have been regarded at best as a dreamer who ought not to be considered seriously. A proposal for an International Bank a few years after the conclusion of the Peace would still have been premature, and would have been doomed to failure. Had the proposal been delayed for another few years, on the other hand, it would probably have missed its psychological moment, as Europe would have adjusted itself to the changed conditions as best it could, and the need for an exceptional remedy involving considerable risks would not have been as pressing.

Post-war Financial History has been characterised by two strong currents: the endeavour to restore monetary

stability through the co-operation of central banks, and
the endeavour to adjust reparations and other claims
arising from the war to realities. It will be seen in the
next two chapters that both currents were moving
towards the establishment of an international organisation of some kind. It was perhaps a coincidence that
both movements, though advancing independently
from each other, should reach simultaneously the stage
when the need for the creation of an international body
had made itself felt more acutely, and when its realisation had come within the realms of practical politics.
The signatories of the Young Report were men with a
sense of reality and no dreamers. They would certainly
have hesitated to put forward a proposal for the
creation of a Bank for International Settlements a few
years ago, but in March 1929 they were satisfied that
the time had arrived for that solution.

The much-debated question whether it is ideas that
shape History, or whether it is the stream of History
that shapes ideas, finds its answer once more in a
synthesis. Without the developments that led up to the
present situation, the idea of an International Bank
would have been rejected, no matter how ingenious the
form it assumed, no matter how convincing the arguments of its authors. On the other hand, though the
situation has matured sufficiently to make the plan
acceptable, it would not have materialised but for
the elaboration of a scheme by a group of experts
who coupled imagination with a sense for realities, and
whose prestige as practical men placed them beyond
the charge of being Utopians. Their ideas, put forward
at the right moment and in an acceptable form, have,
doubtless, contributed to make History. They are none
the less the instruments of historical forces which have

prepared the ground for their scheme, and which have induced the nations concerned to accept it.

The circumstances are strikingly similar to those surrounding the creation of the League of Nations. Before the war, it would have been useless to attempt to put forward such a scheme; it was the events between 1914 and 1919 that brought about the conditions which made the establishment of the League possible. And here again the idea had to be put forward by statesmen of prestige in order to be taken seriously. The authors of the Covenant have certainly contributed to make History, but it was the trend of historical evolution that has made their scheme both necessary and feasible.

There is, indeed, a great deal of similarity between the origin, scope, functions and limitations of the Bank for International Settlements and those of the League of Nations. The League was the outcome of the war, the conception of an International Bank was the outcome of the currency chaos of the war and post-war period. The object of the League is to liquidate the inheritance of war and to prevent the repetition of such disasters; the object of the Bank for International Settlements is to liquidate the currency chaos and to prevent any relapse. The task of the League is to safeguard the existing treaties, that of the Bank is to carry out the agreements on reparations. In neither case is the international organisation entitled to alter the treaties except within the limits prescribed in the text of the treaties themselves. The Bank for International Settlements is not designed as a superior authority over central banks, any more than the League is meant to be a super-State over the existing States. The central banks do not intend to cede the new institution any part of their privileges and powers, any more than the members of the League have re-linquished, or intend to cede, to the League any part of their sovereignty. No legal or political power, but the recognition of the necessity to co-operate and the development of a strong public feeling against the disturbers of harmony are the main factors which maintain the League, and it is upon these that the Bank will depend for its existence. The advantages of the Bank for International Settlements are expected to be of the same nature as those of the League, in the financial instead of the political domain. To mention only one: it will establish regular and frequent personal contacts between the heads of central banks, of the kind that the League has established between the leaders of nations. This is a matter of great importance. Before the creation of the League, no statesman was able to cross the frontiers of his country to meet another statesman without arousing suspicion and irritation in some part of the world. The League meetings now provide an opportunity for them to meet at regular intervals without any such undesirable consequences. The Bank for International Settlements is intended to provide the same facilities for heads of central banks.

As to their weaknesses and limitations, both League and Bank for International Settlements are exposed to the pitfalls of political intrigues. Their important decisions are liable to be governed largely by the necessity of political compromise. Their ability to serve the best interests of mankind is likely to be handicapped, therefore, by political cross-currents and undercurrents. In spite of this, they are capable of rendering valuable services.

It is easy to fall into extremes when judging the

importance of the establishment of the Bank for International Settlements. The one extreme is represented by that small group of idealists who regard the creation of the Bank as marking a new era in human progress. In their imagination, they foresee the growth of a super-Bank of unprecedented magnitude and power, which will attain in time a predominant position in the direction of the financial destinies of mankind. The notion of an International Bank suggests to them an international gold reserve to unite the existing monetary stocks of gold; the issue of a uniform international currency in the place of national currencies; the pooling of all credit resources and their redistribution according to a schedule prepared to meet the respective requirements of the participating countries; the fixing of a "World Bank Rate" which is to become a predominant factor in the international money market. They hope that the activities of the Bank will cause a period of unprecedented international prosperity, by fostering the development of the immense natural wealth and resources of unexploited countries. They include among the labours of the new financial Hercules the reconstruction of Russia and China, a task too big for any but an International Bank. They have gone even further in their imagination. They ascribe to the new Bank the rôle of a supreme international arbitrator, not only in questions of finance and economics, but even in political questions, as the possessor of monopolistic powers in the distribution of credit resources. The Bank, they hope, could distribute rewards or punishments by granting or withholding credit, and would thereby become the guarantor of international peace.

The idea is magnificent—but it is not banking.

Those who expect the new Bank to become all that and more lose sight of realities. There is no reason to hope or to fear—whichever the case may be—that our generation would witness such developments.

It is not only enthusiastic adherents who view the Bank with such exaggerated ideas, but also its fierce opponents who, for the same reason, are frightened by the latent powers of the spirit evoked by the Paris Conference. The other extreme is represented by those who minimise the importance of the Bank, either because they think that it is not worth the trouble spent over it, or because they believe that, if it cannot do much good, it can, at any rate, do very little harm. In their view, all the Bank is meant to do is to fuse the existing Dawes organisations with the existing system of co-operation between central banks. They think that it will be hardly more than an office of reparations payments and a meeting-place of central bankers.

The actual position of the Bank will probably lie somewhere between the two extremes. It is difficult to see, however, at the present stage, how far either extreme will be right. The fact is that not even the authors of the scheme know how the Bank will develop. Never before has anything of the kind been attempted. At this stage it is impossible to prophesy the exact or even the approximate limitations of the possibilities of the Bank. It may begin its work in a modest and unassuming way, and indeed it would be a grave mistake to launch out at once into too ambitious schemes. It may gradually put forth its powers and develop into a most important institution. Time only can show how far the hopes and fears of its friends and foes are justified.

There are at least as many people who fear and oppose the new institution as there are people who welcome and admire it. Just because it is difficult to foresee its functions, none of the existing financial institutions know what to expect through it. Some central banks may fear that the new institution may overshadow them in their own spheres, and may encroach upon their jealously guarded control over the management of the monetary affairs of their country. Some commercial banks are inclined to regard it as a potential rival for deposit and credit business. Some acceptance houses see in it a potential rival in the financing of international trade. Some issuing houses fear that they may lose part of their business as a result of the activities of the new Bank. The natural dislike of vested interests towards any aggressive newcomer is complicated by their vague fear of a supreme authority, as yet undefined, against whom, they imagine, it will be difficult to compete on equal terms.

The idealist adherents of the scheme regard with indignation as narrow and selfish all who look at the problem from that angle. They maintain that the benefit mankind as a whole will derive from the activity of the Bank will be so immense as to counterbalance any sacrifice of individual interests. They hold the opinion, at the same time, that there is no need to talk of sacrificing the interests of any existing bank, for, taking the long view, all banks are bound to benefit by the general advantages obtained through the creation of the Bank. The greater stability will reduce the risk attached to banking, and greater prosperity will increase the possibilities of profit.

Again, opinions are divided between those who fear that the Bank will become a power independent of the Governments to which it owes its existence, and those who are concerned lest it remain too much under the

control of the political authorities. If the fears of the
former were justified, it would infringe the power of
Governments; should the latter be better prophets,
questions of finance would be settled on political
grounds, and Board meetings of the Bank would become
the battlefield of political intrigues and controversies.

Another point on which general uncertainty prevails
is the proposal for an international gold clearing
system. It is difficult to define the precise object of the
scheme; whether it aims at the monopoly of gold transactions; or at the elimination of the physical displacement of gold; or merely at the saving of the expenses of
shipments of the kind which are undertaken by central
banks even at the present time. It is an open question
whether the new Bank will aim at interfering with gold
arbitrage by means of confining exchange movements
within limits narrower than those fixed by gold points.

Over and above all, it remains to be seen how far the
super-Bank will make use of its immense facilities for
credit expansion. This is the aspect of the scheme which
deserves the most attention, as it opens up a vista of
alarming possibilities. The scheme itself is sound, and
it is far from its authors' intention to make of the
Bank a means for international credit inflation. But
then, the bank scheme of John Law was also in itself
sound. The question is whether the new institution will
be tempted to use its resources for financing schemes
as bold as the Louisiana venture whose failure contributed to the downfall of Law. The creation of "new
possibilities for commerce" is one of the objects of the
Bank, as defined in the Report of the Young Committee, and this phrase may easily be regarded as giving
sanction to adventures outside the normal scope of
banking. It also remains to be seen whether the scheme

of our modern John Laws—however sound their intention may be—will not be brought to shipwreck by political interference in the management of the Bank. The spirit of the Duke of Orleans and his *entourage* may survive, although in the changed circumstances it may assume a different form.

The statutes of the Bank, in themselves, do not give any adequate answer to the questions raised. Everything depends upon the interpretation given to these statutes in practice, and upon the manner in which the Board of Directors makes use of its wide discretionary powers. The chapters which follow attempt merely to indicate some of the problems which the new institution is likely to encounter. They give a critical analysis of the plan of the Bank, and enumerate some of the alternatives in its development.

CHAPTER II

CO-OPERATION BETWEEN CENTRAL BANKS

THE year 1923 witnessed the culmination of the post-war crisis in European finance. Monetary conditions exhibited a picture of desperate chaos. Both France and Germany were paying the price for the Ruhr adventure in the depreciation of their currencies; the franc dragged with it the other two "Latin exchanges", while the slump of the mark contributed to the demoralisation of Central and Eastern European currencies. It was rare to find a budget on the Continent which was properly balanced. Budgetary deficits, currency inflation, depreciation of exchanges, rising prices, increasing expenditure were chasing each other in a complete disorder. It was impossible for any of the former Continental belligerents to raise an external loan so as to break that vicious circle. The few experiments with such issues resulted in a failure, discouraging further attempts. Even the countries which had remained neutral during the war were, to some extent, swimming with the tide, instead of assisting in the restoration of normal conditions by maintaining their finances on a sound basis.

In those dark days of the post-war financial crisis of Europe, the sign of dawn was the stabilisation of the Austrian exchange. The credit for this is due to the League of Nations, for it was under the auspices of the

Finance Committee of the League that a reconstruction scheme was elaborated and put into operation, and to the Governments which, by relinquishing the priority of their claims and by guaranteeing a portion of the Reconstruction Loan, enabled Austria to obtain the funds required for the stabilisation of the krone. It is necessary, however, to recognise the great importance of the advance granted by the Bank of England to the Austrian National Bank for the purpose of maintaining the stability of the exchange during the transition period between the conclusion of the agreements for the reconstruction scheme and the actual issue of the loan. Without this advance, the exchange would have continued to depreciate, which would have jeopardised the success of the reconstruction scheme.

The support granted by the Bank of England to the Austrian National Bank was the first public act of co-operation between central banks after the war. The idea of co-operation between banks of issue of different countries is by no means new; it existed already before the war, one of the most conspicuous examples being the support given by the Bank of France to the Bank of England during the Baring crisis. During the war, there was, of course, some co-operation between the Allied central banks and also between the Reichsbank and the other banks of issue of Germany's allies. It was not until after the war, however, that a systematic movement began, with a view to facilitating the stabilisation of currencies. It was largely, if not exclusively, due to the initiative of Mr. Montagu Norman, Governor of the Bank of England. He has fulfilled a historical part, the importance of which cannot be sufficiently appreciated. It was largely through his personal friendship with the late Mr. Benjamin Strong, Governor of

the Federal Reserve Bank of New York, that the
United States was gradually induced to co-operate to
some extent—financially if not politically—in European affairs. Most of Mr. Norman's work for reconstruction was done behind the scenes, and, owing to
his dislike of publicity, neither his contemporaries nor
posterity will be able to judge the full significance of
his activity.

The movement of co-operation began as a one-sided
support of the weak banks by the strong ones, but
gradually developed into a system of reciprocal support. It began as the alliance of a select group of leading institutions, but gradually came to include almost
all European central banks. Nor was it confined to
Europe. Apart from the Federal Reserve system—and
more particularly the Federal Reserve Bank of New
York—which played a leading part in it from the very
onset, the Japanese and Egyptian banks of issue were
also included. A number of central banks which availed
themselves of the support were soon in a position themselves to help others in co-operation with the group
that gave them assistance. Although it was one of the
unwritten rules of the movement that only central
banks on a gold basis should participate, on several
occasions central banks of countries with inconvertible
paper currencies were also admitted. The tendency
pointed towards the inclusion of all central banks within
and outside Europe.

There were two main objects in view of those
directing the movement. The one was the support of
economic reconstruction and monetary stabilisation.
The other was the prevention of a scramble for gold
by central banks. There was also a secondary object,
which was a means to an end rather than an end itself,

i.e., the establishment of closer business relations between central banks. At the same time, the co-operation of central banks also helped to solve the problem of the reparations transfers.

Although the prominent part played by the League of Nations in the economic reconstruction is generally known, comparatively little has been written of the highly important part played by the central banks which joined forces to that end. The above-mentioned case of the Austrian reconstruction duly illustrated the significance of the services rendered. The advance placed at the disposal of the Austrian National Bank enabled Austria to benefit by the loan months before it was actually issued. Even after the issue of the Reconstruction Loan, the Bank of England continued to support the Austrian National Bank by placing funds at its disposal. Similar services were rendered to the Hungarian National Bank. It is understood that the Bank of England returned the interest paid on its advances to these institutions, for the benefit of their pensions fund.

In the case of both Austria and Hungary, the support was given by the Bank of England alone, without the co-operation of other central banks. When Germany's turn came, however, a group of central banks was formed to support the Reichsbank by means of placing capital at the disposal of the Gold Discount Bank. The number of participants continued to increase as there were more and more banks in a position to help others. The stabilisation of the Belgian franc, the lira, the zloty, the drachma, etc., was carried out through the aid of the credits granted by the growing group of central banks. This time, there was no question of an advance, merely of a credit to be drawn upon if and when necessary for the purpose of maintaining the stability of the exchange. In the case of the restoration of the gold standard in Great Britain, the support was granted exclusively by the Federal Reserve system.

Although the efforts of central banks were generally conducted within the framework of the League of Nations schemes, on occasions they acted independently. In the case of Poland, for instance, a scheme was worked out without the assistance of the League of Nations. Nevertheless, the Bank of England lent its support, and participated with a considerable amount in the credit arranged by a group of central banks for the Bank of Poland. The same was the case in the Rumanian stabilisation scheme. Notwithstanding the fact that the Rumanian Government gave its preference to the Franco-American scheme and that the Bank of England was in favour of a League of Nations scheme, the latter took a due share in the credit arranged for the National Bank of Rumania.

Similar credits were granted in the case of the stabilisation of the Bulgarian and Estonian currencies under the auspices of the League of Nations. In the case of Greece, the settlement of refugees from Asia Minor and other parts of Turkey was financed to a great extent with the aid of advances granted by the Bank of England. The Bank of Danzig has also been largely supported by the Bank of England, especially during the early stages of its career.

Although the merits of the work of co-operation between central banks in the restoration of stability in Europe are incontestable, their action did not escape occasional criticism. They were reproached with being too dictatorial towards the countries which needed

their support. It was probably for this reason, and
also because it was considered a sign of inferiority
to be supported by such means, that several countries, which were able to do without the support of
the group of central banks, obtained support from
other quarters. For example, the Danish National
Bank stabilised its exchange with the aid of credits
granted by Hambros Bank and American banking
interests. The Bank of Spain preferred to deal with
Anglo-American banking groups headed by the Mid-
land Bank and Messrs. J. P. Morgan & Co. It was said,
and not without reason, that the principles of the
Finance Committee of the League—which were largely
inspired from Threadneedle Street—were too dogmatic, and failed to take into consideration the difference between a financially developed and undeveloped
countries. The insistence of the authorities, for instance, in the case of Bulgaria and Estonia, that the
central banks should be controlled by private shareholders instead of the Government has caused both
countries considerable inconvenience, as it was not in
accordance with local conditions. In the long run,
however, the countries concerned are likely to benefit
by the rules imposed upon them contrary to their
immediate convenience, not only for the private control of the central banks, but also for the detachment
of business which was not within the sphere proper
to a central bank. Although conditions in some countries are not sufficiently advanced for a pure central
bank, the establishment of such an institution under
foreign pressure will itself accelerate the progress
towards more developed conditions.

Beneficial as the dictatorial methods of the Finance
Committee and the group of co-operating central banks

were, the countries in need of their assistance have gradually become less and less inclined to submit to them. In cases of emergency, they may reluctantly consent to accept dictation from outside. The more conditions approach the normal the less are they likely, however, to accept interference inconsistent with their dignity. It has therefore become desirable at this stage to devise arrangements whereby the countries wanting support could participate in the authority which determines the terms of the support. To ask for and receive assistance would thereby become less humiliating, and unpopular terms would become more palatable. This is one of the *raisons d'être* of the Bank for International Settlements.

Admittedly, the assistance given by central banks to countries desirous of stabilising their currencies was not prompted exclusively by considerations of pure philanthropy. It was to the interest of the countries on a gold basis that the greatest possible number of countries should adopt the gold standard. If there are only two free gold markets they have to stand the full burden of fluctuating demand, while if there are a number of comparatively free gold markets the burden is more evenly distributed and the principal gold markets are relieved of part of the pressure. Up to now, however, this benefit has not shown itself to any noteworthy extent, because most central banks which have returned to the gold standard have been buyers rather than sellers of gold, in order to replenish their reserves. Thus, while in the long run the initiators of the movement of co-operation will benefit by their action, for the time being they suffer from the additional demand for gold of central banks which they assisted in their task of restoring the gold standard.

C

This brings us to what is the second principal aim of the movement of co-operation: the regulation of demand for gold by central banks, in order to avoid a scramble. Most central banks are authorised to include foreign exchanges into their gold reserves, but there is a tendency on the part of most of them gradually to replace these currencies with actual gold. In possession of considerable balances in foreign centres—especially in London and New York—they are well able to draw upon the gold resources of these centres. Although the principal holders of gold are willing to assist these central banks in their endeavour to build up their gold stocks, they have a natural desire to prevent any sudden demand upon their own resources. Even in the case of New York, the coincidence of heavy withdrawals by a number of foreign central banks could be embarrassing. In the case of London, even a comparatively small withdrawal by central banks is inconvenient, because of the narrow margin with which the Bank of England has for some years been working. An understanding has therefore been reached by which central banks undertake not to withdraw any gold from each other without each other's consent. The same principle governs the earmarking and release of gold held by the Bank of England and by the Federal Reserve Bank of New York on account of foreign central banks.

The principle of non-interference with each other's gold reserve has also been extended to the South African gold dealt with in the open market in London. This gold has always been regarded as the natural source from which the Bank of England replenishes its supply. For this reason, the other central banks have agreed not to make any purchases without the consent of the Bank of England, which carries out their buying orders on their behalf. Whenever the gold is stated "to have been acquired for undisclosed destination" it is understood that the buyer is the Bank itself but the purchase was made on account of another central bank. It is to the interest of the central banks themselves that their demand for South African gold should be co-ordinated, so as to avoid competition, which would force them to pay a higher price. The order in which their requirements are met in the market is determined by agreement with the Bank of England, which takes due care of the interest and susceptibilities of all of them. For instance, knowing the harmless rivalry that exists between the Austrian National Bank and the Hungarian National Bank, the Bank of England en-deavours to get equal amounts for both institutions.

This co-operation worked satisfactorily as far as the central banks of small countries are concerned. An example to show how far the spirit of co-operation is carried was provided by the gold purchases of the Bank of Poland in August and September 1929. Although sterling was then at a considerable discount in relation to the dollar and it would have been cheaper to buy the gold in London, the Bank of Poland met its requirements, amounting to about £1,000,000, in New York, overpaying to the extent of thousands of pounds, out of consideration of the difficult situation of the Bank of England.

Unfortunately, the same considerate attitude has not always been noticeable on the part of all central banks. The principal offender against the co-operation has been the Bank of France, which withdrew from the Bank of England and purchased in the open market considerable amounts in 1927. An understanding was reached at the conference of central banks held at

Washington in July 1927, when the Bank of France agreed to abstain from making any purchases without the consent of the Bank of England. Since then there have been no direct purchases by any central banks (either from the Bank or in the market) which could be regarded as a violation of the principle of co-operation.

In spite of this, the state of affairs is far from ideal. There is nothing in the agreement between central banks to prevent the withdrawal of gold by means of special transactions disguised as commercial transactions. In fact, the source of the embarrassment of the Bank of England in the summer and autumn of 1929 was due exclusively to such transactions carried out by the Reichsbank and subsequently by the Bank of France. Although it is difficult to ascertain the exact extent to which either of these institutions was responsible for the withdrawals of gold from London, there is no doubt that had the spirit of the Washington agreement been followed, and not merely the letter, most of those withdrawals would never have taken place. The German withdrawals were officially defended on the ground that they were not objected to by the Bank of England, while the French withdrawals were explained as being the natural consequences of the withdrawal of private balances from London, towards which the Bank of France adopted an attitude of strict neutrality. In an ideal co-operation, more is wanted than mere neutrality towards obviously unnatural gold movements tending to embarrass another central bank. It is, thus, plain that co-operation has not reached perfection. The Bank for International Settlements will have, therefore, an opportunity in this respect also to fulfil a useful task.

An auxiliary means by which central banks have been co-operating is the establishment of closer business relations with each other. Before the war there was fairly close co-operation between the central banks of the members of the Latin Monetary Union and between the Scandinavian central banks, made necessary by the regulations of their respective monetary unions. Apart from that, business relations between central banks were the exception rather than the rule. The Reichsbank conducted most of its London business through the London branch of the Deutsche Bank, while other central banks also preferred to make use of banking connections other than central banks. When after the war new central banks were established or the existing ones were reconstructed, the Bank of England requested them to agree to give, on a basis of reciprocity, exclusive representation in Great Britain. The existing accounts of central banks were transferred to the Bank of England. This has caused considerable ill-feeling among the joint-stock banks and financial houses which were thereby affected. The foreign central banks themselves were also reluctant to give up old-established connections which worked to their satisfaction, all the more as the facilities offered by the Bank of England did not always meet their requirements to the same extent as facilities offered elsewhere.

It was considered desirable, however, from the point of view of closer co-operation, that the accounts of central banks should be concentrated in the hands of each other. A number of central banks did not fall in line with these requirements. The Bank of France is the most conspicuous exception. As it controls substantial resources in London, it works with a large number of banks. On the whole, however, it may be said that business relations between central banks are much closer than before the war. On the Continent, central banks have established accounts with each other. For the first time in their history the Reichsbank and the Bank of France recently established accounts with each other. The Reichsbank has introduced a system facilitating the transfer of funds from one country to another through the intermediary of central banks. Most European central banks, whether or not on a gold basis, have joined this arrangement.

Another auxiliary function of the co-operation of central banks was to facilitate the task of the Agent-General for Reparations Payments of the transfer of funds. Little is known of the arrangements that have been made behind the scenes to secure the smooth working of transfers. The fact that Mr. Parker Gilbert frequently participated in the conference of central banks indicates that the association of the movement of co-operation with the reparations problem was fairly close. About this, however, more will be said in the next chapter.

Although the movement of co-operation of central banks has rendered invaluable services to the progress towards restoration of normal conditions, its shortcomings have been evident. It is at once too informal and too vague in character. Its agreements have no binding force and may easily be given too vague an interpretation. Its working is too casual and clumsy. Although the heads of central banks are anxious to maintain personal contact, the meetings are very few and far between, and are far from representative. Moreover, the movements of prominent bankers are followed closely by the international press, and exaggerated importance is occasionally attached to them. When the object of a journey of a bank governor is merely to discuss routine business as to co-operation, many people are inclined to scent something of great importance, such as loan negotiations. The secrecy with which the movement is surrounded is, admittedly, largely responsible for this state of affairs.

The need for the creation of an organisation which would systematise the co-operation of central banks has been felt for some time. From the point of view of the co-operation of central banks, such an organisation presents the following advantages:

(1) It places co-operation on a systematic basis. At present there are no definite rules to govern it, no definite list of participants, no meetings at fixed intervals. The new organisation would replace the casual character of the movement by a systematic movement.

(2) It provides a central administrative organisation. At present there is no body engaged in organising and co-ordinating the movement. Although the members are likely to wish to retain their authority upon matters of principle, such an administrative body is certainly needed for routine work.

(3) It facilitates personal intercourse of central bankers. While in the course of the movement they only met about once a year, the new organ would provide an opportunity and a necessity for frequent meetings.

(4) It will help to establish discipline among central banks. Although the body will have no power to enforce its decisions any more than the League, its existence will none the less reduce the number of violations of the principles. To accept the ruling of the Bank

is less humiliating than to submit to the decision of individual central banks or groups of central banks.

(5) It will render the movement more efficient. Much waste of time in the arrangement of credits, etc., can be avoided.

(6) It may result in the restriction of the scramble for gold, and it may offer a means to counteract the falling tendency of the international price level.

(7) It will tend to increase the number of countries on a gold basis. Being excluded from participating in the share capital of the Bank will be a stigma of inferiority, and for this reason every central bank will be anxious to qualify for admission.

(8) It will facilitate the exchange of statistical and other information.

It is thus obvious that, apart altogether from every other consideration, the interests of the movement of co-operation itself would justify the establishment of a central organ.

CHAPTER III

PROBLEM OF REPARATIONS

BEFORE the war the international movement of capital assumed the shape of a fairly systematic flow from countries possessing a surplus to countries whose requirements exceeded their own supply. A comparatively small number of countries—in the first place Great Britain, and to a less extent France, Germany, Holland and Belgium—exported their surplus of capital to the economically undeveloped countries, such as the British Dominions, Latin America, China, Russia, Turkey, etc. The payment of interest and principal often assumed the shape of fresh borrowing. Apart from cases where political or financial difficulties affected the credit of borrowers who were unable to raise funds to meet maturities, everything went smoothly. The distribution of capital and the redemption of debt were gradual processes, and did not disturb the international money market to any substantial extent.

Conditions underwent a fundamental change after the war. Germany is compelled by the Treaty to make huge reparation payments, while the Allied nations have to repay the amounts they borrowed from Great Britain and the United States. The necessity of such debt payments has introduced a new factor in the foreign exchange market the importance of which

is occasionally considerable. The principal exchange
which is affected by them is, of course, the Reichsmark,
but it would be a mistake to underestimate its effect
on the currencies of other countries which have to make
such payments.

It is characteristic of the spirit in which the Treaties
and subsequent agreements were made that no apparatus whatever was provided for the purpose of dealing
with this exceptional factor. The transfers of reparation payments were allowed to take care of themselves,
no matter what their effect upon the exchanges. This
lack of foresight was largely responsible for the currency
chaos which followed the Peace Conference.

It is impossible to ascertain the extent to which the
Ruhr adventure was responsible for the final collapse
of the mark, but there is reason to believe that it
merely accelerated an inevitable process. The necessity
of making huge payments and the inability to borrow
abroad would in any case have brought about a collapse of the exchange, though without the effect of
passive resistance in the Ruhr the decline would have
been more gradual.

The Dawes Committee in 1924 fully realised the
necessity of putting an end to this state of anarchy.
The Dawes Plan provided machinery to regulate the
transfers of reparations payments so as to inflict upon
the mark exchange the least possible harm. The Agent-
General was charged with the collection of reparations
and the choice of the most opportune moments for
their transfer to the Allied creditors. Another apparatus, the Transfers Committee, was set up with the
object of stopping transfers as soon as they endangered
the stability of the Reichsmark.

This system was incomparably better than the

régime of complete anarchy in reparations transfers. The German Government was relieved of the responsibility for transfers; its duty in respect of reparations was confined to making payments in Reichsmarks. The Agent-General, in co-operation with the leading central banks, arranged the transfers so as to cause the least possible inconvenience in the foreign exchange markets.

As the application of the Dawes Plan coincided with an unprecedented inflow of foreign funds into Germany, the efficiency of the system established in 1924 did not undergo a real test until early in 1929, when external borrowing was checked. It soon became apparent that Germany could not continue to make reparations payments for any length of time unless it was made possible for her to borrow abroad at the same time. Thus it appeared that the fact whether or not the transfers of reparations payments disturbed the exchange depended not so much on the efficiency of the organisation of transfers as on fluctuations in the international loan market. But for the replacement of the Dawes Plan by the Young Plan, the clause of the former providing for the suspension of transfers might have had to be applied in order to avoid another collapse of the Reichsmark.

It is obviously undesirable that the continuity of reparations transfers should be made dependent upon such fluctuations in the international loan market. To some extent this is unavoidable, especially so long as the payments exceed considerably Germany's normal resources. The influence of the caprices of the capital market can be moderated, however, by means of the co-operation of central banks to facilitate transfers. So long as there is no central organisation to direct this co-operation, it would be a slow and cumbersome pro-

cess to enlist the support of all central banks to assist
Germany during a period of transfer difficulties. To
overcome this disadvantage, the continuous existence
of an organisation equipped with the powers proper to
that purpose is necessary. The same organisation is
destined to act as trustees for reparations payments,
and to assist in the commercialisation of reparations
payments as well as in the financing of deliveries in
kind.

A change in the system of reparations payments was
also made necessary by the greater weight which
Germany had come to occupy in international relations.
Immediately after the war, Germany was regarded as
a nonentity in international politics, to be subjected
to any humiliation by her late enemies. This attitude
reached its culminating point in the Ruhr adventure.
Since 1924 Germany has been making immense progress towards the restoration of her political prestige.
She was admitted to the League of Nations in 1926, and
was immediately given a seat on the Council among
the other leading Powers. Once more her voice carries
considerable weight in international conferences. In
such circumstances, it was politically impossible to
maintain a humiliating system of control, such as had
been established by the Dawes Plan. That system had
its justification in History, both from an economic and
a political point of view, as an intermediate phase. By
the march of events the need for its revision became
evident. Naturally enough, the German Government
was as anxious to be relieved of this reminder of its
recent political inferiority as to terminate the Rhine-
land occupation.

The obvious alternative to the control established
by the Dawes scheme appeared to be a return to the

state of anarchy that existed previous to the London Agreement of 1924. Although the amount of the annuities had been reduced to more normal figures, it would none the less have been hazardous to resort to a complete *laissez-faire* in the matter of transfers. The problem before the Experts Committee in Paris was to find a solution consistent with the dignity of Germany, without, at the same time, causing trouble in the foreign exchange market. One possible solution would have been the establishment of a Transfers Office—a reconstructed Reparations Commission upon which Germany would possess a seat. The predominantly political character of such an organ would have made it, however, hardly an acceptable solution from a German point of view. It was necessary to form an institution which should be non-political in form at least, and in which, if possible, neutral countries should also participate. It was also considered desirable that the institution to be established should confine its functions, as far as transfers are concerned, to assisting the German Government if and when it became necessary, leaving the responsibility for the transfers with the debtor nation.

The necessity for the establishment of a special international organ for the management of reparations payments has thus coincided with the necessity for the creation of an organ for the co-operation of central banks. It was, therefore, the natural consequence of the trend of evolution when in the spring of 1929 a plan was put forward for the combination of the two purposes in the same body. As we pointed out in the previous chapter, central banks had during the past few years been forced to concern themselves in the problem of reparations transfers. From this point of view, therefore, the difference between the old position and the new will be largely one of degree.

As the object of the co-operation of central banks is to regulate anything tending to disorganise exchanges, they should extend their activities over all war debt payments. It is, therefore, desirable that the new Bank should take charge not only of reparations but also of inter-Allied debts. Although less troublesome than reparations, the transfers required by these payments are also large enough to cause inconvenience to the international markets, and their regulation by the new Bank would be a progressive step. The combination of inter-Allied debts and reparations would also have the advantage of lessening the humiliating character of the latter for Germany and other nations which have to pay reparations. No special provision has been made to extend the Bank's scope in this direction, but the organisation is clearly fitted for it, and is likely to be applied accordingly sooner or later.

The combination of the functions of a central office for central banks with those of an office for reparations payments has been severely criticised on the ground that it combines two morally and materially incongruous matters. The point has been made that, whereas co-operation between central banks is a product of idealism, the endeavour to exact reparations is a survival of a spirit of hostility. It has been feared that the one will prove incompatible with the other. But reflection makes it impossible to regard the problem in this way. Reparations, it is true, are an unpleasant inheritance from the war, and the sooner the world is rid of them, as well as of inter-Allied debts, the better. This does not mean, however, that the handling of reparations payments would compromise the institution which has for its object to bring nations together in friendly co-operation.

It is most unlikely that either of the two currents which have together created the plan for the Bank would have been strong enough by itself to overcome the general hostility of public opinion and official circles against bold innovations. A Reparations Bank, with its task limited to receiving and distributing reparation annuities and other functions associated with reparations, would be merely another name for the combination of existing reparation authorities. The movement of central banks is not sufficiently known or appreciated outside the circle of those directly concerned to enable its leaders to obtain sufficient support for its concentration into an International Bank. The combination of the two purposes was, therefore, a necessary evil. It is, moreover, a temporary state of affairs; reparations will not go on for ever, while it is to be hoped that the existence of the Bank will be permanent.

CHAPTER IV

THE BANK PLAN IN THE YOUNG REPORT

WHEN in March 1929 the Committee of Reparation Experts announced its intention of suggesting the establishment of an International Bank, a section of public opinion was inclined to interpret the statement as an indication of the failure of the Conference to arrive at a solution of the main problem of reparations. It was believed that the Committee, having arrived at a deadlock upon the task for which it was summoned, was trying to save appearances by producing an agreement on a side-issue. Newspaper comments declared that the establishment of such an organisation would not in the least contribute to the solution of the problem as to the transfer of reparations payments: all it could do would be to combine the existing reparations organisations, and to give them a new name. This interpretation of the announcement was, however, hardly justified. It would do less than justice to the experts to suppose that they put forward the Bank scheme as a last refuge in order to avoid having to acknowledge their complete defeat. In fact, an agreement upon the Bank by itself would have been valueless without an agreement on the reparations problem as a whole. Although it constitutes the most important innovation as compared with the Dawes scheme, it would not have been practicable without a general agreement on the wider issues.

Undoubtedly, in the course of the vicissitudes of the Paris negotiations, there were many moments when it seemed that a deadlock had been reached. But the Bank scheme was not intended to mask the failure of the Conference. The introductory remarks of the Young Report give an acceptable explanation of the process by which the Conference was led to the conclusion which elaborated the Bank scheme as part of the reparations scheme. The experts realised the difficulties of estimating the limits of Germany's capacity to pay, without knowing whether or not there would be an adequate organisation to deal with situations of emergency. In other words, a higher figure for the total sum payable as reparations would be more acceptable to Germany if provisions were made for obtaining temporary relief without either having to depend upon lengthy and complicated diplomatic procedure or having to submit to any humiliating form of control. To the creditors a reduction of the annuities was more acceptable if it was compensated for by the creation of an organisation calculated to increase the possibility of the payment of these reduced annuities. Thus, before continuing the discussion of the amount of conditional and unconditional annuities, it was found advisable to determine the nature of this organisation.

It is, of course, true that, in itself, the Bank does not solve the problem of transfers. But the character of a Bank for International Settlements seemed to offer a more hopeful solution than any alternative scheme. Such an institution might, to some extent, increase Germany's capacity to pay, and might help to improve the efficiency of the reparations system. The advan-

tages of the inclusion of the Bank scheme in the Young
Plan, from the point of view of reparations, may be
summarised as follows:

(1) By unifying the existing clumsy, complicated
and cumbersome reparations organisations, it simplified the whole reparations problem. The elimination of
some of the organisations set up by the Dawes scheme
should result in economy in expenses. The concentration of all functions connected with reparation
payments in the hands of one single body is more eco-
nomical and more efficient. A Bank is more suitable
than any other organisation to act as trustee for the
reparations payments.

(2) It will be of great help in the commercialisation
and mobilisation of the reparations debt. Once the
principles on which the commercialisation may take
place are laid down, it is necessary to have a permanent organ to carry out the mobilisation of the
debt as and when opportunity arises. Although the
Bank will have to consult with the Governments
concerned before undertaking the mobilisation of any
part of the debt, it is a much simpler procedure than
the negotiation of an agreement through diplomatic
channels. Considering that any delay may result in
the missing of the psychological moment for such
transactions, the importance of a permanent and
business-like organisation in charge of the matter
cannot be sufficiently emphasised.

(3) It will play an important part in the direction,
control and financing of deliveries in kind. By granting advances to the firms engaged in making such deliveries, it will greatly facilitate these operations.

(4) It will provide an authority able to advise the
creditor Governments as to the German Government's

declaration of its inability to continue the transfer of postponable annuities. It would perhaps have been desirable, from the point of view of the debtor, that instead of appointing a special committee for that purpose, consisting only of the experts of countries directly concerned, the Board of Directors of the Bank itself should have been authorised to fulfil this function. But such a solution would have accentuated the political character of the Bank, which had to be avoided.

(5) It will give Germany assistance to avoid the necessity of suspending transfers, if her difficulties appear to be of a temporary nature. Under the Dawes scheme, temporary difficulties—such as were experienced in the spring of 1929, when temporary factors caused a depreciation of the Reichsmark and resulted in a heavy efflux of gold—may necessitate the suspension of transfers; while under the Young Plan assistance in the form of credits would be provided for such cases.

(6) It will take charge of the investment within Germany of Reichsmark payments made by the German Government during the period of suspension of transfers.

(7) It will create additional facilities for German exports by facilitating the reconstruction of certain countries and the fresh development of others. Upon this subject the wording of the Young Plan is rather vague, and it gives no indication whatever as to the schemes that its authors may have had in mind.

(8) It will contribute, out of its profits, towards the payment of the last 22 annuities. Whether or not these profits will be of import it is impossible to foretell. Should the activities of the Bank attain a very large

scale, the profits accumulated at compound interest may provide an important contribution towards the relief of Germany from her reparations debt.

(9) It will reduce considerably the political character of the reparations problem, though few people will agree with the Young Report that it altogether eliminates the political element.

(10) It has increased neutral elements in the administration of reparations. While some of the appointments made under the Dawes scheme were neutral, from this point of view the composition of the Bank's Board and its shareholders represents distinct progress.

(11) It will tend to improve financial relations between former belligerents, by the establishment of a permanent link between their financial authorities. Personal intercourse between the heads of central banks of political rivals will tend to lead to a better understanding.

(12) It may prevent a fall in the international price level and may thus avert a corresponding increase in the burden of reparations and inter-Allied debts.

The plan produced by the Young Committee, though incomparably superior to the Dawes scheme, is far from ideal. Possibly, and even probably, it is not the final solution of the reparations problem, but it provides the means for testing the application of the reduced annuities within the next few years.

The Young Plan discriminates between what are the essential and obligatory functions of the Bank, namely, those connected with reparations, and its auxiliary or permissible functions, which are largely the continuation of co-operation between central banks.

The Report recognises, however, that no clear distinction is possible between the two sets of functions, because the first leads naturally into the second, on account of the necessity of assisting Germany in case of temporary transfer difficulties and of creating additional facilities to increase her capacity to pay. The Paris experts foresee a gradual increase in the relative importance of the auxiliary functions of the Bank, and express their belief that a time will come when these functions will overshadow the reparation functions for which the Bank was primarily created.

Without minimising the importance of the Bank as a channel for the liquidation of reparations, it seems that, for the business community, the so-called "auxiliary functions" are by far the more interesting and important. The change in the system of reparations mainly concerns Governments. It does not directly affect the business world or the man in the street, nor does it excite the imagination of the public. On the other hand, the international banking activities of the institution are calculated to exercise a direct effect upon the actual financial situation, and upon the system of international financial intercourse. Owing to the complete uncertainty of the extent and the nature of this activity, it attracts much more interest, even outside the business world, than the reparations functions which have their well-defined limitations.

The non-reparations functions of the Bank, as foreshadowed by the Young Plan, are discussed in detail in the next chapter.

Annex I. of the Young Report indicates the outlines of the organisation of the Bank for International Settlements, and will remain, notwithstanding subsequent modifications, the foundation upon which the detailed structure of the Bank has been built. It deserves, therefore, special attention.

Part I. applies the name as "Bank for International Settlements", instead of "Bank for International Payments", as was originally suggested. The choice of the name is satisfactory, in that it covers the reparations functions of the Bank, without emphasising them specifically, so that the original name can be retained after the reparations functions have ceased. An alternative would have been to call the Bank simply the "International Bank", but, because there are already several banks with that title, the choice of a new name was desirable.

The purpose of the Bank is declared to be to provide additional facilities for international financial relations and to assist the administration of the Young Plan. The terms are sufficiently vague to allow the extension of the Bank's activities should circumstances make it desirable. No provision was made for the location of the Bank, because the experts were unable to come to an agreement at the Paris meeting.

Part II. deals with the share capital, which is fixed at the equivalent of $100,000,000, of which 25 per cent is to be paid up. At first sight, a sum of £5,000,000 may appear as inadequate for the initial capital of a bank of the importance of the Bank for International Settlements. It indicates, however, that the authors do not wish the Bank to embark upon unduly ambitious schemes at the very start. The distribution of the shares between the various countries is calculated to retain the control in the hands of the seven countries responsible for the scheme. Other participants may include countries interested in reparations and countries on a gold or gold exchange basis, but their total interest can never exceed 44 per cent of the share capital. Although the central banks who will subscribe the share capital are enabled to pass shares on to the public if they do not desire to keep them as an investment, the central banks will retain the voting right attached to the shares.

Part III. provides for the establishment of the Organisation Committee, on which the seven countries are to be represented on a basis of equality. The task of the Organisation Committee was described as the elaboration of the statutes and charter, and the making of all preliminary arrangements required until the Board of Directors actually takes charge.

Part IV. indicates the scope of the Board of Directors and Management. The Board of Directors are given exceptionally wide powers. They are even entitled to modify the statutes so far as such alteration is not inconsistent with the provisions of the Young Plan. (This power has subsequently been curtailed by the Organising Committee.) The experts, anxious to safeguard the independence of the Bank from political influences, declared that the functions of Directors were incompatible with those involving national political responsibilities. To maintain the essentially European character of the institution, they stipulated that all Directors should be resident in Europe, or should at least be in a position to attend Board meetings regularly.

The composition of the Board is such as to give to the seven original countries a voting strength greater than their participation in the share capital of the Bank. While they are to take 56 per cent of the shares, they obtain 16 seats out of 25 on the Board, which is equivalent to 64 per cent of the votes—

omitting the casting vote of the Chairman. This does not necessarily mean, however, that the interests of the small participants will be sacrificed, as there will seldom be unanimity among the seven principal participants when questions of importance are at issue. Moreover, inasmuch as for every decision of importance a majority of two-thirds is required, the sixteen Directors representing the seven principal countries, even if unanimous, will have to obtain the support of at least one Director representing smaller holders in order to obtain the necessary two-thirds majority.

It is interesting to note that the Board is not meant to consist exclusively of bankers, but is to include the representatives of industry and commerce, in accordance with modern tendencies.

Part V. deals with the various categories of deposits which the Bank is entitled to receive. They include deposits on annuity account from the creditor Governments, ordinary deposits from central banks, deposits on clearing accounts from central banks, consisting of gold, deposits in connection with the Bank's reparation functions, and a special deposit from the German Government. The Bank has the right to pay interest on deposits not liable to withdrawal except on one month's notice. In this respect it differs from many central banks. The rate of interest will vary according to the nature of deposits.

Part VI. is of special importance, as it enumerates some of the operations the Bank is entitled to undertake. The list is by no means exhaustive, and the Board of Directors is entitled at its discretion to include others. Of vital importance is the clause whereby the central banks are entitled to veto any transaction of the Bank in their currency or with their country.

The Bank is entitled to buy and sell gold coin and
bullion, which may be interpreted as an indication
that the authors of the scheme had in mind the
establishment of a gold reserve. It is also entitled to
earmark gold on account of central banks, which fore-
shadows a scheme of international gold clearing. The
Bank may deal in bills and other short-term obligations, it may open deposit accounts with central banks,
may rediscount bills presented by central banks, may
make advances to central banks on security, it may
buy and sell long-term securities (other than shares).
It may issue obligations which have investments in
Germany as collateral security, or other long- or short-
term obligations of its own. The terms of this article
are rather vague, and provide no safeguard against
the possibility of competition with existing banks.
The only restriction specifically mentioned, in addition to the veto of central banks, is that which forbids
the Bank to acquire a predominant control over business interests in any country. If the Young Report
had included provisions limiting the Bank's scope—
of the kind which were subsequently included in the
statutes—much of the adverse criticism which followed the publication of the report could have been
avoided.

Part VII. deals with the general aspects of the
Bank's Trustee functions, which are to include the
service of the German External Loan of 1924, the
various certificates and obligations to be issued by
Germany in connection with the Plan, and the service
of annuities. The same article deals with the Bank's
functions as regards deliveries in kind, the convocation of the Special Advisory Committee in case of suspension of transfers. The Bank may act as Trustee

under special agreements, either at the request of Germany, or any creditor Government, or any central bank.

Part VIII. deals in detail with the Bank's functions as depositary for the service of the German annuities. It describes at some length the process of collection and distribution of annuities. While the international banking functions of the Bank are left largely to the judgement of the Board of Directors, its reparation function is subject to precise regulations.

Part IX. deals with the agency functions of the Bank, either on behalf of central banks, or on behalf of creditor Governments desirous of mobilising their share of the reparations bonds. Its relations with central banks are based on the principle of reciprocity ; while in the relation of a central bank with other banks it is always the latter that acts as agent on behalf of the former—being a bankers' bank—in the case of the relations between central banks and the Bank for International Settlements services of the same kind are mutually rendered to one another.

In regard to the mobilisation of annuities, the Bank's task is to advise the Governments whether or not the moment is opportune for such operations, and to get in touch with the central banks in whose countries the issue is to be made. Should a creditor Government wish to issue reparations bonds in its own market only, the Bank's task is confined to the creation of bonds, while the operation is handled by the particular Government concerned.

Part X. determines the reserve requirements of the Bank. Curiously enough, it fixes a minimum ratio such as applies in the case of some central banks ; the percentage fixed by the Young Report is 40 per cent for sight liabilities and 25 per cent for time deposits. As the reserve may include, in addition to gold, short-dated securities in gold currencies, the fixing of a minimum ratio does not seem to have any useful purpose, for the Bank is obliged in any case to hold practically all its assets in the shape of such securities. As the Bank for International Settlements is not a bank of issue, it does not seem necessary to fix a minimum reserve ratio. (The provisions in this respect were omitted from the statutes of the Bank.)

Part XI. deals with the distribution of profits. The shareholders are entitled to a cumulative dividend of 6 per cent, while the maximum dividend they can expect is 12 per cent. After making ample provisions for reserves, the remaining net profits are to be used, to the extent of 75 per cent to remunerate the time deposits of the Government or central banks of the creditor countries or of Germany, and to the extent of 25 per cent to accumulate a special fund for the reduction of the last 22 German annuities, provided that Germany deposits with the Bank 400,000,000 Reichsmarks.

Part XII. contains some general provisions as to the termination of the Dawes régime, the balance-sheet and the auditing of the Bank's accounts, and arbitration in case of disagreement.

Other sections of the Young Plan make also frequent reference to the Bank for International Settlements, when dealing with various aspects of the Plan in which the Bank is to play some part. The importance of the Bank plan in the proposed régime can be measured by the space its description occupies in the Young Report.

CHAPTER V

SCOPE OF THE BANKING DEPARTMENT

WHILE the duties of the Bank in the handling of reparations—which will be carried out by its Reparations Department—are strictly defined, the Young Report is rather vague as to its tasks in the general field of international banking, which will be carried out by its Banking Department. The exact nature of the services it can usefully perform in that direction will be ascertained by experience. It is, nevertheless, possible to form a general conception as to the principal tasks it is meant to fulfil. The statutes of the Bank give little positive information, but there are some fairly clear indications in the Young Report as to what were the intentions of the authors of the scheme. It is necessary to emphasise that those who credited them with the intention of trying to produce a miraculous remedy able to heal our present-day economic evils do not do justice to their sense of reality. The work marked out for the Bank is work of a sort that is already being performed to some extent by existing organisations such as central banks and the League of Nations. The difference will be one of degree rather than of kind, so long as the Bank's activities do not overstep the limits planned for them by the authors of the scheme.

It is, of course, possible that, under a too ambitious management, the Bank would disregard the intentions

44

of its originators, and would embark upon adventurous schemes, or would lose its sense of proportion as to the extent to which its expansion is sound and safe. We propose to deal with these possibilities in another chapter. Here we confine ourselves to the normal functions of the Banking Department.

The following are some of the most obvious tasks which lie within the scope of the Bank:

(1) Assistance to countries wishing to restore the gold standard.

(2) Assistance in the maintenance of a gold standard in case of emergency.

(3) Assistance in the relief of temporary pressure.

(4) Establishment of an international gold clearing system.

(5) Regular collection and exchange of information upon the international monetary situation.

Although many countries have restored the gold standard since 1925, either through their own efforts or with the aid of central banks and the League of Nations, there is still much left to be done in this direction. Countries which have yet to achieve legal stabilisation of their currencies are Spain, Portugal, Brazil, Yugoslavia, and Turkey; the Bank could perform invaluable services in assisting them. It is most desirable that this task should be left to the Bank, and that individual central banks should not compete with it in this respect. There has already been too much rivalry between central banks in the past—inspired by political or other considerations —to play a prominent part in the financial reconstruction of certain countries. Once there exists a special organ in which all leading central banks participate, which has for one of its main tasks the assistance of the stabilisation of currencies, any attempt by a particular central bank to secure a moral stronghold in any country by undertaking the stabilisation of its currency should be inadmissible, as it would necessarily be detrimental to the interests of the new institution and to the spirit of co-operation which is the *conditio sine qua non* of its success.

As the departure from gold standard of any country which had returned to it exerts a demoralising effect and tends to create distrust towards the stability of the gold standard in other countries, it is of a great importance that, in any cases of emergency, the Bank should come to the rescue. The Young Plan makes it the duty of the Bank to assist Germany if difficulties arise, and points out that the case of Germany is by no means the only opportunity before the Bank. It is much easier to obtain support that is urgently wanted from the Bank than to be forced to organise specially a group of central banks for that purpose.

While the support of the Bank should be employed in the first place to relieve emergency when the stability of a currency is in danger, it should also serve as far as possible to bring relief in less extreme cases. Those countries in which there is imminent danger of the suspension of the gold standard should have a prior claim to the support of the Bank, but, so far as possible, countries suffering from any temporary embarrassment which does not amount to emergency should also benefit by its assistance. In fact, it is to be hoped that, after the restoration of international financial stability, cases of emergency will be very rare, and the support of the Bank will be used as the normal means to assist central banks to meet seasonal pressure upon the exchange or any other inconvenience. As commercial banks regard their re-discounting facility with the central bank as the ultimate means, to which they only resort if other means are exhausted, similarly central banks should regard the Bank for International Settlements as their last resort.

Formerly it was believed that the establishment of an international clearing system would necessarily involve the establishment of an international gold reserve. The statutes of the Bank provide, however, the means for such a clearing system without the creation of any central gold reserve. The Bank is authorised to accept gold deposits on account of central banks, and also to earmark gold in the vaults of central banks on its own account. It is thus possible to have an international gold reserve without establishing a central gold reserve. The Bank of England may, for instance, deposit £10,000,000 of gold on the books of the Bank, while the latter may leave the gold with the Bank of England. This system will facilitate the transfer of gold from one central bank to another without having to make actual gold shipments. Chapter X. will deal in greater detail with this subject.

Although the central banks which have been associated in the movement of co-operation have interchanged statistical and other information—there was even an informal conference in Paris in 1928 to regulate this interchange—there has hitherto been no central authority to collect and distribute the material, and to examine it from an international point of view. The new institution will fill a distinct gap in this respect.

Apart from the tasks of the Bank which have been enumerated, there are others which are less obvious but which may become none the less feasible in the course of time. The following are a few examples:

(1) To undertake the administration of all war debt payments.

(2) To take an interest in the financial reconstruction of Russia and China.

(3) To assume the rôle of trustee for all debt services under international control—for instance in the case of the Greek external debt.

(4) To appoint financial advisers to Governments and central banks.

(5) To assume the control of the arrangements to prevent the counterfeiting of bank notes.

(6) To publish precise information as to the practice of various central banks in the matter of gold shipments.

It is disappointing that the Young Plan did not include among the duties of the new Bank the administration of all inter-Allied debts. The reason for this is that every Government is desirous to retain its freedom of action in that respect. But it would be perhaps possible to find a solution which did not interfere with their freedom of action and yet secured for the Bank the possibility of marshalling the transfers to the best advantage of all parties concerned.

The question of the financial reconstruction of Russia under the existing régime is delicate and complicated, and cannot be considered apart from the sore question of the settlement of old claims. The time may come when a formula is found by which the Soviet Government will undertake the payment of an agreed compensation, provided that the creditor countries assist it in the task of duly increasing its capacity to pay. No institution would then be more suitable to undertake the transactions required than the Bank for International Settlements. It would necessitate, of

course, the admission of the State Bank of the U.S.S.R.
to participation in the Bank. Possibly some time may
have to elapse before conditions are such that this can
be regarded as practical politics.

As for China, once civil war has ceased it will
be necessary to assist the Chinese to reorganise their
country. Although the currency is not on a gold basis
—and from the point of view of international monetary
stability it is hoped that she will be in no hurry to
adopt it—the new Central Bank of China may eventually be admitted to some form of participation in the
Bank for International Settlements. Chinese opinion
would be probably more willing to submit to some
form of control when the time comes for the country's
monetary reconstruction if the control were exercised
by an international authority in which the Chinese
Central Bank also participated.

Once the Bank is established and has surmounted
the initial difficulties, there is no reason why a gradual
expansion of its operations should not be undertaken.
There are at present a number of international financial
organisations which could perform their duties much
more favourably under the auspices of the Bank. For
example, the Caisse Commune of Paris or the International Financial Commission of Athens should be
merged into the Bank. There is no need, however, to
hurry forward such expansion. In the beginning, the
management will have sufficient difficulties in organising the immediate activities of the Bank and it would
not be desirable to complicate its task any further until
it has settled down in its work.

As the Bank is expected to take charge of the
stabilisation of the few remaining unstable currencies,
the appointment of financial advisers or observers is

E

another logical outcome of its task. Being less political than the League of Nations, possibly advisers appointed by the Bank would be more welcome in some countries than those named by the League.

The international bureau established in Vienna for the prevention of counterfeiting bank-notes should be brought under the auspices of the Bank, whose close associations with banks of issue would assist it in that task.

At present very little is known as to the technical details of the rules applied by various central banks in buying and selling gold. As gold arbitrage will remain in existence notwithstanding the establishment of an international gold clearing, it would be of great assistance to banks if the details were to be made available from time to time. In addition, the publication of other technical details as to central banks' practice would also be useful.

The allusion of the Young Report to the Bank's task of opening up new fields for commerce leaves a wide scope for imagination. Possibly it may merely refer to the anticipated increase of international commercial activity as a result of the stabilisation of currencies. The statutes exclude the possibility of acquiring shares or of taking a controlling interest in business undertakings, so that there can be no question of any direct participation in enterprises aiming at the creation of new markets for export trade. As the opening up of new countries requires long-term investments, the Bank is hardly suitable for that purpose, though it may assist any scheme by supplying the short-term funds required, once the long-term capital has been provided for. Such ventures are necessarily of a speculative nature—they would bear a too strong resemblance to John Law's

"Mississippi Venture"—and it would be contrary to the spirit of the principles on which the Bank is based if it were to take any risk that a central bank would not be prepared to take.

The non-reparation functions of the Bank will contribute to bring about a more equal distribution of the world's financial resources as between various countries. They will tend to eliminate the abnormal discrepancies between interest rates that developed since the war. Over and above all, they will tend to stabilise the international price level, and to counteract a general and prolonged decline of prices. They will thus render a great service in the restoration of normal conditions. Through improving the spirit of co-operation between central banks, the Bank will be instrumental in a regulation of the demand for gold; by such means, and through expanding or contracting credit it may be in a position to influence world prices.

CHAPTER VI

THE Conference of The Hague confirmed the principle of the establishment of the Bank for International Settlements, and left the elaboration of its details to the Organising Committee which met at Baden-Baden in October. The task of the Organising Committee was anything but easy. First of all, they had to settle the highly controversial question of the location of the Bank, about which more is said in the next chapter. Apart from this, they had to reach a compromise between the necessity of leaving the Board of the Bank a comparatively free hand and satisfying those who considered it essential to define as exactly as possible the scope of the institution. As the Bank is entirely without precedent, it is in the nature of things impossible to draft hard and fast rules to determine its exact sphere of activity. The rules will have to grow from the experience of the institution; to tie it down within too narrow limits would be equivalent to preventing it from developing its natural scope.

On the other hand, there is the legitimate fear of vested interests that the new institution will become a formidable rival. Hence the desire to exclude it from certain branches of activity. The Young Report emphasised that the Bank is so designed that it will not interfere with the functions performed by the existing

52

institutions, but it is to cut out for itself supplementary functions in a special field of its own. This was not sufficient, however, to reassure banking interests, which claimed more specific guarantees against the competition of the new Bank. They maintained that even if the authors of the scheme did not intend to develop the Bank into a rival of the existing banks, their desire might be disregarded in practice unless it were embodied in the statutes.

It was, of course, impossible to include in the statutes a clause to the effect that the Bank should not compete with existing institutions, for such a clause would have paralysed its activities altogether. Certain clauses offering safeguards against competition have, however, been inserted; they are calculated to reassure vested interests to some extent, though they are far from sufficient to eliminate their fears altogether.

One of the interesting departures of the statutes from the Young Plan is the inclusion of a list of transactions from which the Bank is debarred. The first commandment shatters the dream of those few idealists who hoped that the Bank would issue international currency, because it prohibits the issue of notes to bearer. Even if a scheme of an international currency could be worked out on paper, conditions are certainly far from sufficiently advanced. To link up an Utopian dream with the practical and feasible objects of the Bank would be to compromise the scheme in advance.

The Bank is also forbidden to undertake acceptance business. This will doubtless reassure the acceptance houses, which were at first alarmed by the possibility of the appearance of a new and powerful rival. At the present time, acceptance business is probably the most competitive branch of banking, and, as a result of keen

competition, commission rates have declined although
the risks attached to it have increased. It is only
reasonable, therefore, to treat that branch with discrimination, and to exclude the possibility of any competition on the part of the new Bank. Moreover, the
authority of granting acceptance credits would open
immense possibilities for credit inflation. In any case,
as the task of the institution is to re-discount bills from
the portfolio of the central banks and not to introduce
the habit of drawing bills by central banks, the prohibition does not in any way handicap its normal
activities. Its relations with firms other than central
banks will be the exception rather than the rule, and
its freedom of action will not suffer, therefore, to any
extent by the restrictions.

It would be a mistake to imagine, however, that the
exclusion of the Bank from acceptance business would
in itself technically prevent it from competing with
banks in the financing of foreign trade. The Bank will
be entitled to establish contact with foreign banks,
with the authorisation of the central banks of the
countries concerned, and it is in a position to discount
their bills. Although in highly developed countries the
central banks would probably object to such practice,
in countries anxious to encourage the influx of foreign
capital no objection is likely to be raised. Thus, it is
possible for the Bank to finance foreign trade by dis-
counting bills, thereby diverting business from acceptance houses. It would be a grave error, however, if
the Bank were to resort to such direct competition.
If it is desirous of supporting a country in need of
foreign funds, it is in a good position to give all the
support required through the intermediary of central
banks. The result would be, of course, practically the

same: for if they enable the central banks to finance a larger portion of the foreign trade of their countries, they will thereby divert business which would normally have found its way to acceptance houses and to banks engaged in acceptance business.

The restriction preventing the Bank from granting acceptance credits is thus more apparent than real. The ultimate result is the same whether the Bank grants direct acceptance credits or whether it re-discounts some of the bills held by central banks, enabling them to increase, in turn, the limit of re-discounting facilities granted to the banks in their countries. The competition is, however, less obvious and less aggressive, and is calculated to provoke less hostility on the part of vested interests. It is left to the management and Board of the Bank to use their powers of competition with discretion. The primary object of the Bank is not to provide for a more equal distribution of the world's financial resources, but to support a currency in case of emergency. In doing so, they cannot help competing to some extent with banking interests, but there is no justification for going further in that respect than is inevitable in the interest of international monetary stability.

Another restriction aims at preventing the Bank from establishing with Governments any relations other than those originating from its rôle in connection with reparations. The Bank is not allowed to open current accounts for Governments, though it is allowed and will even encourage the opening of time deposit accounts; and it is forbidden to grant any loans to Governments. As for the latter, it can be circumvented by the acquisition of Treasury bills. The Bank is at liberty to buy or discount short-term obligations of

Governments which are currently marketable. It is also entitled to grant to central banks loans secured by short-term Treasury bills. Thus, here again it is the spirit rather than the letter of the rules by which it is hoped that the Bank will be prevented from taking an interest in the financing of Governments. As central banks are most anxious to prevent such practices, they are in a position to veto any transaction with the Government of their country even though in accordance with the letter of the statutes.

The original Young Report imposed a restriction on the acquisition of the control of any business interests in any country. This restriction has been confirmed and amplified by the statutes, and has been supplemented by a clause prohibiting the acquisition of real property other than that required for the Bank's own purposes. While the restriction on acceptance business is calculated to reassure financially advanced countries, this latter restriction is for the benefit of countries in a comparatively backward stage, where public opinion may object to the possibility of the acquisition of land and other vital resources by the international banking trust.

Another most important modification of the Young Report by the Organising Committee is the qualification of the right of central banks to veto any transaction in their country or in their currency. If the veto is unrestricted, it would mean that any central bank could object to the withdrawal of funds invested by the Bank in their country, which would, of course, immobilise the Bank's resources and interfere with its freedom of action. The result of such legal situation would probably be that the Bank would not invest its funds in any currency unless the central bank undertakes not to veto their withdrawal at any time.

The restriction of the veto considerably reduces its significance. After all, it is only in exceptional cases that central banks would object to the inflow of funds. Had the Bank existed in 1927, the Bank of France would probably have vetoed any attempt to invest its funds in francs, as it found the influx of foreign funds rather embarrassing. Had it existed in 1928 and 1929, the American authorities would probably have objected to any transfer of funds to the United States, as it would have been contrary to the monetary policy they pursued. In the great majority of cases, however, an influx of funds is welcomed, while their withdrawal is very often viewed with disfavour. The question is whether, notwithstanding the restriction on the veto, the Bank will be at liberty in practice to withdraw its funds from any country whenever convenient. Should the withdrawal cause inconvenience to the central bank concerned, its request to the Bank would be almost as effective as a veto: for, after all, the Bank is intended to avert such emergencies and not to create them. At present there is no legal means whatever to prevent the Bank of France, for instance, from withdrawing all or a great part of its funds invested in London and New York. If it abstains from doing so it is because it wants to avoid causing embarrassment to either of these markets. It is most unlikely that a Bank established for the purpose of assisting the co-operation of central banks would be less considerate in this respect than the institution which has been regarded as the principal offender against the principles of co-operation.

The veto may serve a useful purpose on occasions when the central bank of a country is anxious to maintain tight money conditions. It may also be used with benefit to prevent the Bank from investing its funds in

certain types of securities. For example, if a central
bank is anxious to develop a bill market and the supply
of bills is inadequate, it would be unwise to allow the
Bank to buy up the whole supply, as it would prevent
the development of a regular demand.

The statutes provide for the conclusion of special
arrangements between the Bank and the central banks
authorising the former to carry out certain types of
business without any further steps to obtain the
latter's permission. Such arrangements would be
indeed highly desirable, for the necessity of obtaining special permission for every transaction would
paralyse the activities of the Bank.

Another important point in which the statutes
depart from the rules laid down by the Young Report
is the omission of the clauses as to a minimum percentage of reserve ratio on sight liabilities and time
deposits. The fixing of such ratio by the Expert Committee was based on a misconception of the scope and
nature of the Bank's activities, both from a theoretical
and a practical point of view. From a theoretical point
of view, the Bank, not being a bank of issue, should be
under no obligation to keep a minimum reserve ratio.
From a practical point of view, as the minimum reserve
may include, apart from gold, any short-term claims in
approved currencies, there is no object in fixing a
minimum percentage, as the Bank has to keep almost
all its assets in such form that its reserve will not be
much short of 100 per cent in any case. It would make
a considerable difference if part of the reserve had to be
kept in gold. But such a measure would be highly
undesirable both from the point of view of general
interests—as it would accentuate the scramble for gold
—and from the point of view of the Bank's earning

capacity. While it is only reasonable to expect a bank of issue to keep some of its assets in the form of non-interest-bearing security, it would hardly be fair to inflict such a burden on the Bank for International Settlements, which does not enjoy the benefit of being able to loan its own notes on which it need pay no interest. The decision of the Organising Committee to waive the minimum reserve requirements was, therefore, fully justified.

At the same time, however, it may well be asked whether it would not have been advisable to make some kind of provision for establishing some kind of reserve ratio, so as to fix a limit to the possibilities of credit expansion. This aspect of the problem will be dealt with in detail in Chapter VIII. on "Credit Resources of the Bank".

The statutes confine themselves to emphasising the necessity of maintaining the Bank's liquidity and enumerating the assets which may be considered as liquid. They also point out that, in determining the proportion of the Bank's assets which may be invested in any particular currency, the Board is to pay due regard to the distribution of the bank's liabilities. This cannot, of course, be regarded as a hard and fast rule, for its literal application would mean that the Bank can lend to any country only the amount it borrows from it, in which case there would be little benefit in its activities. It means, however, that, apart from special cases in which the Bank's support is required, it should hold its balances as far as possible in the currencies in which its liabilities are expressed. Thus, if various central banks transfer some of their sterling balances to the Bank for International Settlements, the latter will have to keep these funds, as far as possible, in their original form instead of transferring them into another currency.

The importance of this interpretation of the statutes is particularly great during the transition period. It is hardly likely that in the beginning any central bank will part with any substantial part of its gold reserve to deposit it with the Bank. In order to establish contact they will probably transfer part of their foreign exchange reserves to the Bank. The wholesale transfer of sterling reserves would cause considerable inconvenience if it were to be accompanied by their wholesale conversion into another currency. In the long run, the London market would probably lose some of the foreign balances which it is in a position at present to re-lend to its customers, but the loss is not likely to be either sudden or substantial.

There is a marked tendency in the statutes to emphasise the international character of the Bank—as compared with its character of a Reparations Bank—to a greater extent than the Young Plan. It slightly altered the possible composition of the shareholders by laying stress on the desire to include the greatest possible number of central banks, and by enabling the Board to include additional central banks with full voting right on the occasion of future capital increases. It curtailed to a great extent the powers of the Board of Directors, on which reparations Powers have a stronger representation than at the shareholders' meeting, by depriving them of their authority to alter statutes. While according to the Young Plan vacancies on the Board are to be filled by the nominees of the representatives of the seven founder banks only, according to the statutes the decision rests with the whole Board.

The question may arise whether it would not have

been advisable to include in the statutes provisions as to the voting rights of shares subscribed by central banks which abandon the gold standard, or which fail to pay their debts to the Bank. It may be argued that it was wiser not to meet trouble half-way by making provisions for such unpleasant cases, as it would disclose a lack of confidence in the success of the Bank's efforts. After all, the Bank is established largely to prevent central banks from having to suspend the gold standard or from getting into difficulties. In spite of that, a clause providing for the suspension of the voting right of the shares of the offenders would not have been out of place. Another point which could have usefully been dealt with in the statutes is the attitude of the Bank in case of a war. This matter is discussed in greater detail in Chapter XI., which deals with the political aspects of the scheme.

The Hague Conference of January 1930 passed the Statutes practically without alteration. The only modification made was in Article 20, the purpose being to give a more precise definition to the right of central banks to veto any transaction on their market or in their currency. It is gratifying to record the fact that politicians abstained from interfering with the work accomplished by the financial experts of the Organising Committee, as far as the Statutes of the Bank were concerned.

The Charter and Trust Agreement elaborated at Baden-Baden underwent, on the other hand, substantial modifications at The Hague. It was necessary to modify the former, so as to make it acceptable to the Swiss Government. The Trust Agreement had to be modified in compliance with the wishes of the various parties concerned.

CHAPTER VII

THE point on which the experts found it most difficult to agree was the choice of the city which should be the headquarters of the Bank for International Settlements. As a matter of course, every nation would have welcomed it on its own territory, not only because of the material advantages involved, but also for reasons of prestige. It was obvious that the conflicting claims for the headquarters of the Bank could not be settled by financial considerations alone. From the point of view of the success of the scheme, the ideal solution would have been to establish the Bank in the centre which offered the most technical advantages as the site of an institution of that kind. The requirements of such a centre are the following:

(1) It should be a financial centre of some importance, with lively international banking activity.

(2) It should possess a good foreign exchange market, with adequate facilities to transact business in every important currency.

(3) It should possess a good gold market, with ample supplies and a regular demand, and a complete freedom of gold movements.

(4) It should possess a good bill market.

(5) Its geographical position should be advantageous, with special regard to the intercourse with New York.

It is obvious that no other centre satisfies these requirements to the same extent as London. If the matter had been considered from a purely financial point of view, the choice would have fallen upon London without hesitation. The reasons why London is more suitable than any other centre for the housing of the Bank are the following:

(1) It is still the most important international financial centre in the world, with an unparalleled banking organisation to transact international business, supported by experience and traditions. From that point of view, no other centre can be compared with London. New York may, for the moment, possess larger resources for lending overseas, but its international banking organisation lacks experience, and the mentality of the market is predominantly provincial and not international. Paris may possess, for the moment, ample liquid resources for lending overseas, but her total external resources are much smaller than those of this country. In any case, her international banking organisation leaves much to be desired, and its development is handicapped by a mentality which renders business on an international scale rather difficult. Amsterdam possesses international banking organisation and also international spirit, but it compares unfavourably with London as to resources and the extension of its international activities. Berlin has comparatively little international business. The same is true of Brussels, while from an international point of view neither Milan nor any Italian centre deserves consideration. Switzerland transacts a great deal of international business, but it is divided between Zurich, Basle, Geneva and Berne.

(2) London possesses an excellent foreign exchange

market, with a highly developed technical organisation and well trained staff. Although certain Eastern
European currencies may have a better market in
Paris or in Switzerland, their importance is comparatively small. London's superiority in the market for
dollars, on the other hand, is incontestable, and
that is the currency which matters more than any
other. London is, moreover, in an almost monopolistic
position in Europe as regards Latin American and
Eastern currencies, and has the actual monopoly of
most of the exchanges of the British Empire. Wherever
the Bank is situated it will have to transact any business in these currencies *via* London, so that it would
have simplified matters to establish the Bank in
London itself.

(3) London possesses the only gold market where
there are regular supplies of gold in addition to the
reserves of the central bank. For the moment the
gold stock of the Bank of England compares unfavourably with those of the Federal Reserve banks
and the Bank of France. But this is obviously a temporary state of affairs. After all, Great Britain is still
the largest creditor nation, and, by realising some of
her foreign investments, is well in a position to draw
gold. As the Bank is not meant to be established for a
year or a decade, but as a permanent institution, it is
the long view that matters. There is no doubt about
it that, in the long run, the Bank of England will be
as well in a position to part freely with any amounts
of gold without inconvenience to the market as any
other central bank. Moreover, the regular free supplies
of gold will also continue to come to London, wherever
the Bank is established. Owing to its close political,
commercial, and financial association with London,

and owing to the exceptional transport facilities to this centre, South Africa will always continue to send her surplus gold to the London market, where it can depend on a regular demand.

It is, moreover, not at all certain that central banks possessing gold stocks larger than ours will part with gold as freely as the Bank of England in all circumstances. Their willingness to part with gold has not undergone a real test since the war. Although the Federal Reserve banks possess huge surplus stocks, even now there is some uneasiness when French withdrawals assume large dimensions. As for the Bank of France, before the war it had the reputation of handicapping by various means the free outflow of gold. The franc is at present at a premium, and there is a huge foreign exchange reserve to support the exchange if necessary, so that the willingness of the French central institution to carry out the letter and spirit of its gold standard cannot be tested for some time. Considering the exceptionally difficult situation of the Bank of England during 1929, and the willingness with which it nevertheless parted with gold, it may be safely stated that in the long run London is a better gold market—even apart from the supply in the open market—than either New York or Paris. It possesses, moreover, houses specialising in gold transport which do not exist in any other centre.

(4) London's superiority as a bill market is so generally known and admitted that this point needs no further arguments. It is, in fact, the only really good bill market in the world. Notwithstanding all efforts, New York is still inferior to London, and will remain inferior so long as the market for loans to brokers remains the principal facility for short-term

F

investment of funds. The French financial authorities
are endeavouring to establish a bill market in Paris,
but there are a number of technical as well as psychological obstacles, and while the former may be elimi-
nated in a few years, it may take generations to overcome the latter, if they can be overcome at all. The
Amsterdam bill market is about the best on the Continent, but it cannot be compared to London. As for
Switzerland, the system of discrimination adopted by
the National Bank against bills financing foreign trade
between two foreign countries makes the development
of an active bill market impossible.

(5) London's geographical position may not be as
advantageous from the point of view of intercourse
with Continental countries as that of some Continental
centres—especially Switzerland—but it is certainly
more advantageous from the point of view of the intercourse of Europe with other continents in general and
with the United States in particular. It would be a
mistake to regard the Bank as being destined to remain
an essentially European institution. Admittedly European interests predominate—although American and
Japanese interests are also well represented—but its
natural evolution points towards the establishment of
a world bank. No Continental centre, nor even New
York, is in such an advantageous geographical position
as London as the clearing house of the world. Mail routes
and cables from East and West converge upon London
to a greater extent than upon any other single centre.

In addition, London has a stronger claim than any
other centre to house the head offices of the Bank also
on moral ground. Having been the financial centre of
the world for many generations, it has a justified claim
to regard that position, with its privileges and burdens,

as its personal property. The establishment of the Bank in any other centre tends to weaken London's position to some extent, while it does not affect the position of other centres which cannot lose what they have never possessed. Thus, the centre receiving the Bank will gain largely at the expense of London. As there is no special British interest attached to the establishment of the Bank, there was no reason why Great Britain of all countries should sacrifice part of the advantages it possesses for the sake of it. Had the centre been established in London, it would have merely confirmed the existing state of affairs. As it is established elsewhere it gives a present to some country which has no more claim than any other country to receiving such a gratuitous gift.

The advantages attached to the possession of the head offices of the Bank cannot be ascertained in advance, as nobody knows into what the institution will develop. It is exactly because of this uncertainty that it would have been desirable to secure the head offices, in case it should develop into something of predominant importance. As far as can be seen at present, the main advantages, in order of their probability, are the following:

(1) As the head office of the Bank will employ hundreds of well-paid clerks, and will result in the visit of foreign bankers, it contributes to a small extent to the prosperity of the town and the country in which it is situated.

(2) As it will carry on a certain amount of foreign exchange transactions, it will contribute to the development of the foreign exchange market.

(3) As it will buy and sell gold, it will create an active gold market.

(4) As the chances are that a comparatively large proportion of its assets will be held in the currency of the country where it is located, it will contribute to the development of the local bill market and money market.

(5) As the presence of the Bank enhances the importance of the centre, it constitutes a psychological factor tending to result in an all-round increase of its international activities.

(6) It is a matter of prestige to possess the head offices of the World Bank, apart altogether from its material advantages.

It is thus not surprising that there has been such keen competition to obtain the head offices of the Bank. For the moment the Bank is predominantly European, and is concerned with reparations which are an essentially European affair, and therefore centres in other continents, such as New York or Tokio, were never seriously considered. From the very first, the claim for establishing the head offices in London was put forward in the British Press, but official circles did not seem to have attached sufficient importance to it. The British monetary authorities have been credited with the opinion that, as the Bank itself will be little more than an administrative office, and everything essential will be decided by the Board, it does not matter where it is located. Mr. Snowden did not make any effort at The Hague to secure the head offices for London, although he would have then been in a position to obtain such a concession from the other parties involved.

Although in some quarters in France there was a strong desire to secure the Bank for Paris, the French Government itself did not press the point particularly, except so far as it was desirable to oppose the British claim. The main efforts of the French Government were focussed upon opposition to London. The French official view may be summed up that it does not matter where the Bank was so long as it was neither in London nor in Berlin nor in Italy. As Berlin and Italy have never been put forward seriously the opposition was directed exclusively against London. The British claim was also opposed by Belgium, because she hoped to obtain the Bank for Brussels. As to Germany, she officially did not oppose London, but there was a very strong current of public opinion against it, because of public resentment against the liquidation of German property in this country after the war. Germany was also determined to oppose Paris to the utmost, but there was no need for any strong action in that direction. On the other hand, it was the German opposition to the choice of Brussels that eventually determined the choice of Basle. As for Italy, she displayed a neutral attitude, though the choice of Paris would have probably irritated her.

The attitude of the interested parties may thus be summed up as follows:

Great Britain.—A strong claim in favour of London, or, if impossible, to accept Amsterdam in the first place and some other small centre in the second place.

France.—To oppose London to the utmost. To oppose Amsterdam on the ground that German influences were strong there. To favour Brussels in the first place and Switzerland in the second place.

Belgium.—A strong claim in favour of Brussels, to oppose every other centre, especially Amsterdam.

Germany.—To oppose to the utmost either Paris or Brussels, to favour Amsterdam and accept any other centre.

Italy.—No particular opposition against any centre, preference for a small centre.

United States and Japan.—To endeavour to conciliate these apparently irreconcilable standpoints.

The Paris Conference of Reparations Experts left the choice of the centre open. The Young Report states that the Bank ". . . shall be located in a financial centre hereafter to be designated. In selecting the country of incorporation due consideration shall be given to obtaining powers sufficiently broad to enable it to perform its functions with requisite freedom and with suitable immunities from taxation." This clause merely determines that the Bank shall be located in a financial centre—a rather elastic notion, which none the less precludes the possibility of placing the Bank in a neutral town of no financial importance, so as to avoid favouring any existing financial centre. As to obtaining broad powers and immunity from taxation, there is no doubt that any Government desirous of obtaining the Bank would be pleased to grant them.

It is understood that, in the course of the Paris Conference of Experts, some vague verbal promises were made to Belgium that the Bank would be given to Brussels. It was trusting in these promises that the Belgian delegates agreed not to insist upon the settlement of the Belgian claim for mark notes (issued during the German occupation) as part of the Young Plan. This promise had no binding force, however, because they were not incorporated in the Young Report, and in any case the Governments concerned did not consider themselves bound by that Report. Moreover, the mark claims were subsequently settled by means of direct negotiations between Belgium and Germany, on terms most favourable to Belgium.

It was hoped that the matter would be settled at The Hague. In fact, it was stated in the foreign press that the firm attitude of Mr. Snowden about the revision of the Young annuities had for object to obtain in compensation for a retreat the head offices of the Bank for London. Unfortunately, this was entirely without foundation. The location of the Bank was not subject to negotiations in connection with the revision of the annuities. After an agreement had been reached on the principles of the Young Plan, then—and only then— the British delegates began to press their claim for a decision on the location of the Bank, but met with opposition from more than one quarter. It was decided to leave the decision to the Organising Committee.

When the Organising Committee met at Baden-Baden, the location of the Bank was the problem which they found it most difficult to settle. It was believed for some time that the article in the statutes dealing with the location of the Bank might have to be left open. Eventually, however, an agreement was reached in the shape of a political compromise. The two extreme solutions of choosing London or Paris were rejected. The two intermediate solutions of choosing either Brussels or Amsterdam met with a similar fate. The latter was not pressed by either of the parties represented. A compromise was reached exactly half-way between the two extremes.

The choice of Switzerland was undoubtedly a political compromise, but even from a financial point of view it is better than some other solutions suggested. In fact, from a British point of view, if not from the point of view of the prospects of the Bank, it is the second best solution. From the point of view of the interests of London, Basle is better than any of the

big centres, especially Paris, and it is decidedly better
than Amsterdam, which is in many ways her rival. It
is also better than Brussels, because of the predominantly French influence and the strong political atmo-
sphere in that city. It will have to operate largely via
London when dealing with other continents, while
Amsterdam, Brussels or Paris would have transacted
a greater proportion of such business direct. Its only
disadvantage from a British point of view is that it is
at a fairly long distance from London. From the point
of view of the Bank, Basle is hardly the ideal centre.
Its favourable geographical position and its political
"neutrality" are practically the only advantages it has.
Apart from that, it is in a less favourable position than
either Zurich or Geneva.

Possibly in the course of time everybody may realise the necessity of placing the Bank in a centre of
first-rate importance. In that case, London's claims
may possibly be put forward with a better chance of
success.

Until experience shows the significance and nature of
the Bank's activities, it is impossible to form an idea
as to the extent to which its establishment in another
centre is likely to affect London's position as an international financial centre. In dealing with this question,
it is necessary to discriminate between temporary and
permanent effects. The establishment of the Bank
may bring about a fair amount of shifting of balances,
as several central banks will transfer part of their
sterling holdings to the new institution. This does not
necessarily mean, however, that the funds would be
actually withdrawn from London. As was pointed
out in Chapter VI., the statutes of the Bank indicate
the necessity of keeping the assets as far as possible

in the currencies in which the Bank's liabilities are expressed.

The situation is somewhat less reassuring as far as the permanent effects of the change are concerned. The Bank, if successful and active, is bound to divert some business from this market, though the extent of the possible loss should not be exaggerated. The proposed gold clearing scheme may also interfere to some extent with London's position as an international gold market, but it is unlikely to cause much harm in this direction. In any case, it is reasonable to hope that the general increase of international financial activity brought about by the Bank will benefit London to a sufficient extent to compensate the City for any loss caused by the establishment of the new institution at Basle.

CHAPTER VIII

CREDIT RESOURCES OF THE BANK

THE extent to which the Bank will be able to supply credit to central banks and to provide support when required is undoubtedly the most interesting aspect of the scheme. It is here that we are confronted with an innovation at least as revolutionary as the bank of issue created by John Law in France in the eighteenth century. The public knows as little about its significance and experts are as puzzled by its possibilities as were John Law's contemporaries. The object of the present chapter is to prove that there are inherent in the scheme for the Bank for International Settlements dangers of a similar kind to those latent in John Law's bank of issue, and to emphasise that nothing but an ultra-conservative credit policy and a fundamentally sound management can prevent the Bank from being the cause of something approaching an international disaster.

Although the Bank will begin business with a paid-up capital of 125,000,000 Swiss francs (under £5,000,000), it will possess from the very first an almost unlimited goodwill and almost unlimited resources. Its actual and potential resources may be enumerated as follows:

(1) Its paid-up capital.

(2) Its callable capital. As the authorised total of 500,000,000 Swiss francs is subscribed by central banks

and guaranteed by the seven founder banks, the un-called capital may be considered as an asset of absolute certainty.

(3) Reparations annuities held until their distribution to the creditor Governments.

(4) The non-interest bearing deposit of 125,000,000 Reichsmarks paid into the "National Sub-Divisions" of the Annuity Trust Account in which the creditor Governments participate in proportion to their percentages in reparation payments.

(5) The German Government's non-interest bearing deposit of an amount not exceeding 100,000,000 Reichsmarks, in accordance with Annex III of The Hague Agreement.

(6) The French Government's guaranteed deposit of 500,000,000 Reichsmarks.

(7) The German Government's deposit of 400,000,000 Reichsmarks. Although there is no absolute obligation on the part of Germany to deposit the full amount, in view of the advantages attached to it she may possibly do so.

(8) Other Governments' five-years deposits. Presumably every one of the seven founder countries will deposit a certain amount, so as to participate in the distribution of the balance of profits.

(9) Central banks' deposits and/or current account balances. There is no doubt that every participating central bank will take the first opportunity to open an account with the Bank.

Over and above these resources, the Bank will possess an immensely wide possibility for expanding credit. It is true that the statutes deprive it of the right to grant acceptance credits, thereby blocking one most important channel through which an excessive expansion of credit might have taken place. In spite of this limitation, the Bank will be in a position to increase its resources to an extent that is entirely without precedent in the history of commercial banking. It can do so in the pursuance of its normal functions of making advances to and receiving deposits from its customers, the central banks. In this respect its position is similar to that of a commercial bank rather than that of a central bank.

It is now generally admitted that a commercial bank is able to increase the amount of its deposits by increasing the amount of the advances it grants to its customers. If a joint-stock bank grants a commercial firm an advance of, say, £1,000,000, most probably the total amount will not be drawn upon, but part of it will be left on deposit with the bank. Of the rest, which goes into circulation, a part will probably return to the bank. The same amount—or at least a great part of it—can thus be re-lent over and over again, and the process results in a marked increase of the total amount of deposits held by the bank. There is no reason why it should be otherwise as far as the Bank for International Settlements is concerned. It will grant loans to central banks on securities specified in its statutes, and the unused balance of the loans will increase its total resources. As in the case of commercial banks, the same amount can be re-lent over and over again, and every transaction increases the total resources of the Bank.

There is one very important difference between commercial banks and the Bank for International Settlements. The expansion of the resources of the former is limited by the necessity of maintaining a traditional ratio of cash to deposits, the observation of which is

one of the fundamental principles of sound banking.
Cash includes gold, notes, and balances with the central
institution. Its amount is largely determined by the
credit policy of the central institution and by the gold
position. Thus, commercial banks are by no means at
liberty to increase the amount of their advances, once
their deposits have swollen to about ten times their
cash holding.

The Bank for International Settlements is restrained
by no such limitations. Even if the traditional ratio
applied by the commercial banks—or possibly a more
conservative figure—is observed, this does not prevent it from expanding credit to a very great extent.
Its cash supply necessarily includes its balances with
central banks, which constitute a very considerable
proportion of its assets. Its liquid assets also include,
however—according to the statutes—all its holdings of
short-term bills, etc.: in one word, almost every asset
they are entitled to hold. This means that the increase
of its deposits brought about by the granting of fresh
advances also increases its liquid assets almost to the
same extent, and this, in turn, would enable the Bank
to grant fresh advances by a multiple of the increase.
The potential lending capacity of the Bank would thus
tend to increase in geometric progression. The process has all the characteristics of an avalanche, unless
checked in time by inherently sound management and
conservative principles.

It may be objected that the Bank would only grant
advances on good security. But a central bank would
find it easy to provide security that satisfies the Bank.
It holds large amounts of genuine first-class commercial bills which would pass for good security,
especially if the central bank endorses them. Moreover,

central banks are in a position to give part of their gold
or foreign exchange reserves in security of advances
from the Bank. Although it is highly anomalous that
the same gold or foreign currencies should serve as a
security both for the note issue of the central bank and
for the advances granted by the Bank for International
Settlements, there have been similar cases in the past
and there is nothing in the statutes of most central
banks to prevent them from making such double use of
their reserves in future. As the Bank would have a prior
claim on those resources, its advances would be well
secured; but it would be anything but fair to holders
of the notes issued by the central bank. As the Bank is
not likely to judge the merits of credit applications
exclusively from the point of view of its own business
interests, but is bound to pay due regard to general
interests, it is hoped that such practice will be dis-
couraged. Otherwise any central bank would be able to
increase its note circulation almost indefinitely by
obtaining an advance from the Bank, depositing with
it the securities acquired with the aid of the foreign
currency thus obtained, raising on the security another
advance, and repeating this process *ad infinitum*.

We do not suggest that the authors of the scheme
have envisaged such an expansion of credit. They are
all sound bankers, economists, and business men, who
would be the first to condemn any rapid credit expansion in their respective countries. Nor it it likely
that the institution controlled by highly conservative
central banks would get a management which would
willingly depart from the principles of sound banking.
But the possibility of inflationary expansion will be
present under the existing statutes, and it is certain
that there will be both temptation and pressure to

induce the Bank to make use of it. As will be seen in the chapter devoted to the political aspects of the scheme, in order to satisfy the conflicting claims of various countries there will always be temptation to make extensive use of the Bank's resources. If country A is given a credit, its political or economic rival, country B, will feel aggrieved unless it also obtains an equivalent credit. It is to be feared that the application of country A for a credit will be opposed by country B and its supporters on the Board unless assurance is given by country A and its adherents that a similar application on the part of country B will be received favourably. There will be a strong inducement to treat everybody favourably, and this cannot be done otherwise than through making use of the dangerous possibility of expanding credit. As the possibility exists, it will be most difficult to resist political pressure.

The situation can best be compared with that of a commercial bank whose Board of Directors consists of representatives of ambitious industrial enterprises, all anxious to expand with the financial support of the bank. As the means of the bank are restricted, the available resources are divided among those who control the bank by a series of compromises. Every application will be resisted by the Directors other than the applicant himself, as there would be less available for the rest if his request is granted. If, however, the bank somehow obtains the means of creating credit, then all Directors are willing to satisfy the requirements of their previous rival applicants, in anticipation of similarly favourable treatment on their part. It is much easier to satisfy a vigorous claim by sinning against the canons of sound banking than to antagonise any of the shareholders or Directors by refusing their application.

The case is purposely presented here in a very extreme form. Unquestionably, any unsound credit expansion will be resisted to the utmost by most members of the Board of the Bank, so that it would be unduly pessimistic to present the danger of a credit inflation as the logical outcome of the system. But exaggeration of this sort is sometimes necessary to draw attention to certain weak points which might otherwise be neglected. Although there is no danger whatever that the Bank will begin its activities by letting loose a cataract of inflation, the existence of such a danger ought to be borne in mind. Perhaps the first step in the wrong direction will be hardly noticeable. In fact, owing to the novelty of the system it will be impossible to define in advance the line which separates sound from unsound credit expansion. It is, therefore, possible that the Bank may gradually drift, unnoticed by the public, by the experts and by its own management, towards dangerous areas, and that, by the time it is noticed, a retreat will become difficult.

The danger is accentuated by the fact that both the Bank for International Settlements and its customers —who are at the same time its shareholders—possess an almost unlimited goodwill. The credit standing of central banks is high, and although the shareholders' liability for the Bank for International Settlements is limited to the uncalled amount of the subscribed capital, in reality there is an unlimited moral liability. Thus, loans granted by the Bank to central banks or by central banks to the Bank, are to be regarded as gilt-edged and equivalent to cash. A pyramid of entries in the books of the Bank will assume the appearance of reality.

To some extent, the credit expansion is justified.

When two strong and solid banks amalgamate, the result is that the limits of the credit of the new institution are usually higher than the total of the two banks previous to their amalgamation. If the leading central banks of all countries establish a bank for which they are all morally responsible, naturally this will tend to produce the same effect, on a larger scale. Within reasonable limits, the judicious use of the new supply of credit is bound to be productive. After all, financial history provides a long series of examples of the transformation of credit into actual goods and services. Moreover, a general extension of credit may appear justifiable if it aims at counteracting a decline of world prices caused by an excessive demand for gold. The problem is to find the limit beyond which it is not advisable to go.

There should be an index designed to signal the danger, which would enable the Board to refuse applications irrespective of political pressure. If a legal minimum gold reserve were to be fixed, that would provide such an index. For reasons of a theoretical as well as a practical nature, however—as indicated in Chapter VI.—the fixing of a minimum gold reserve is not practicable. It would increase the demand for gold, which would render the benefits of the non-reparations functions of the Bank rather problematic. An alternative solution would be to exclude from the category of liquid assets any form of investment apart from sight liabilities of the founder central banks towards the Bank. Apart altogether from the possibility of irritation caused by the discrimination, there would remain the danger of political pressure, as those anxious to obtain credit would insist upon the investment of an unduly large portion of the Bank's assets in that form. There would, however, be a considerable difference in degree as far as the danger is concerned. It might be necessary, therefore, to attempt a solution of that kind. The absurd state of affairs that, whatever business the Bank might do—within the limits of its statutes, of course—it would always be regarded as practically 100 per cent liquid, is untenable. There is no need for any alteration in the statutes in order to apply the principle suggested. After all, though there is no provision in the statutes of the joint-stock banks for a compulsory minimum ratio between cash and deposits, they nevertheless consider it their duty to maintain a customary average. The figure is not rigidly fixed—in the case of the nine clearing banks the percentage declined between the second half of 1927 and that of 1929 from about $11\frac{1}{2}$ per cent to about $10\frac{1}{2}$ per cent; all banks followed, none the less, the same course. No bank is likely to make any reduction in the self-imposed ratio unless the other banks follow the same tendency. It will be essential for the Bank to adopt the same principle.

An alternative solution would be to adopt the Continental method of maintaining a certain ratio between the Bank's own resources (paid-up capital and reserves) and its deposits and other liabilities. As the site of the Bank is in Switzerland, possibly it will follow Continental traditions in this respect. This solution would have the disadvantage of inducing the participants in the Bank to increase the capital whenever a further expansion of credit is wanted. Yet another solution would be to fix the maximum limit of credits to be granted to any central bank, in accordance with the amount of its gold and foreign exchange reserves, excluding the amounts serving as a security for advances.

In the absence of any precedent, it is difficult to suggest any concrete rule to follow, but it is to be hoped that the Board will find an acceptable solution in accordance with the conservative traditions of the banks represented on the Board. What is essential is that there should be an index which would automatically give warning if ever the Bank were about to overstep the limit of sound finance.

CHAPTER IX

THE BANK AND WORLD PRICES

WE have shown in the previous chapter that the Bank for International Settlements possesses—for good or evil—the means of bringing about international credit extension. It is thus in a position to influence to a great extent the tendency of the international level of prices, by means of regulating the amount of its credits to central banks. The exceptional power it possesses is not altogether without precedent. Since the war the monetary policy of the Federal Reserve system has become by far the most important single factor influencing world prices. During the last year or two, its prominence has been somewhat eclipsed by the rising importance of another factor, the gold policy of the Bank of France. As experience has shown that it is possible for an institution to acquire such fatal power it is much more desirable that the power should be held by an international body rather than by any national institution. Thus, far from being disquieting, the possibility that the Bank for International Settlements may exert an influence upon world prices should be regarded as decidedly reassuring.

Although it is unquestionably flattering to the prestige of any central bank to be able to determine by its policy the tendency of world prices, the privilege also carries certain obligations. A central bank in such a position is torn between the desire of serving the interests of its own country and of abstaining from causing inconvenience or embarrassment to the rest of the world. In many cases, these two considerations conflict with each other, so that the central bank is faced with the dilemma of taking the broad international view —in which case it becomes the target of political attacks at home—or serving domestic interest with no regard for the convenience of the rest of the world—in which case it is condemned by international public opinion, a factor which even the most powerful of financial institutions can ill afford to ignore nowadays. Moreover, the hegemony of any central bank in the international money market does not last for ever. The Federal Reserve authorities had to cede that place, in consequence of the events of 1929 in Wall Street, to the Bank of France, while the latter will also be superseded sooner or later. It is thus the best solution in the long run for all parties concerned to come to a compromise and to leave the task of influencing world prices to an international body on which all central banks are represented.

This does not, however, mean that the Bank for International Settlements will become in time the sole institution which has the power of influencing international price level. Apart from the natural and artificial causes of price movements, the conflicting influences wielded by individual central banks will also continue to exist; but the Bank for International Settlements will have a moderating influence upon them.

Although, as was pointed out in the previous chapter, the danger of international credit inflation through the abuse of the Bank's power exists, it is by no means imminent. For the moment it is not international inflation but international deflation that is threatening us. The persistent fall of prices cannot be regarded with indifference either from the point of view of the problem of reparations or from the point of view of general trade conditions. Its continuance is calculated to cause immense harm to every country.

From the point of view of reparations, inter-Allied debts, and other debts, public and private, this is a question of great importance, as the real burden of these debts tends to increase in proportion to the decline of prices. When in June 1929 the German delegates accepted the annuities fixed by the Young Plan as representing the maximum of Germany's capacity to pay, they acted on the assumption that the real burden represented by the figures would remain approximately unchanged. Meanwhile, the average level of prices declined, and the real burden of the amounts increased considerably. Should the fall of prices continue, it may easily lead to a collapse of the Young Plan as a result of an excessive increase of the burden of reparations.

The falling trend of prices is equally detrimental from the point of view of business prosperity. Amongst the several factors which have contributed to the present world-wide depression the fall of prices occupies a predominant place. It is to the interest of both reparations debtors and creditors, and of the prosperity of trade, that the fall of prices, so far as it is artificial, should be checked. Thus, once more the identity of interests of Governments interested in reparations and central banks interested in maintaining prosperity becomes evident, and provides a justification for the creation of an organisation combining the functions of a

Reparations Office with those of the movement of co-operation between central banks.

It will take some time before the Bank is able to develop its powers sufficiently to become a leading factor in the movements of world prices. During the initial stages of its activities, it will have to proceed carefully, and will be too fully occupied with its own infantile troubles to launch into ambitious experiments. The extent to which it will be able to make itself felt will tend to increase gradually, and it is reasonable to assume that, within a few years, it will be in a position to assume the rôle of the principal authority regulating the international price level. The judicious use of this exceptional power is of extreme importance. The best possible intentions may fail to benefit mankind if they are coupled with a dogmatic mentality, and with the worshipping of that idol of the twentieth-century economists: the index number.

It is essential to discriminate between the causes of the fall in prices. The mere fact that the index number shows a decline does not in itself justify a policy aiming at a corresponding increase. If, as was the case during 1929–30, the fall is due largely to natural causes, such as agricultural over-production, it would be a fatal mistake to try to remedy the evil by means of credit expansion. Such expansion would not be in that case a measure against deflation but a decidedly inflation-ist policy. It is only if and when, and so far as, the decline is due to monetary causes that an intervention on the part of the Bank for International Settlements is desirable. If it is an excessive demand for gold that is responsible for a tendency of falling prices then it should be the aim of the Bank to counteract the tend-ency, and to enable the international banking system to maintain an adequate volume of credit in spite of the inadequacy of the volume of gold.

There are several ways by which that end can be achieved:

(1) The Bank can avoid deflation by arranging a systematic distribution of gold between central banks, thereby preventing excessive demand by some of them.

(2) Should it fail to attain this end it can prevent the contraction of credit caused by a scramble for gold, by means of bringing about an extension of international credit resources.

(3) By its mere existence it can make the same amount of gold serve as a basis for a larger volume of credit.

The principal aim of the co-operation between central banks has been to moderate the appetite of some of them for gold, and to prevent an excessive demand from bringing about a fall of prices. As was pointed out in previous chapters, there is every reason to hope that this task can be better achieved by a systematic co-operation through the Bank for International Settlements than the casual and informal co-operation which has hitherto been the practice.

If, in spite of the efforts of the Bank, the scramble for gold continues and brings about a scarcity of gold in a number of leading countries, the Bank will be in a position to prevent deflation by means of transferring some of its resources to the countries concerned, which would naturally affect the world price level. The Bank is also able to check a falling tendency of world prices by an all-round extension of credit.

Even without granting any exceptional support, the Bank can, by its mere existence, enable central banks to make a fuller use than hitherto of their gold reserves.

Hitherto central banks have endeavoured to accumulate a safety margin over and above the legal minimum reserve ratio, so as to be in a position to satisfy a fluctuating demand. In future, the maintenance of such a safety margin will no longer be so essential—and possibly even the legal minimum ratio could be lowered—because the central banks will be in a position to fall back upon the Bank of International Settlements in case of emergency. In determining the extent to which central banks can depend upon its support, the Bank will be able to influence their policy aiming at making the same amount of gold serve as a basis for a larger volume of credit.

Thus, while it is highly essential that the Bank for International Settlements should abstain from an expansion of credit of an inflationary nature it is permissible and even desirable that it should use its resources for the prevention of deflation. In practice, it is admittedly most difficult to draw the line between monetary and non-monetary causes of price movements, as well as between anti-deflationary and inflationary measures. It is desirable that, in case of doubt, the Bank should err on the side of conservatism.

CHAPTER X

A WORLD BANK RATE

NEITHER the Young Report nor the statutes contain any provisions governing the manner in which the Bank for International Settlements shall fix its rates of interest. Both Young Committee and Organising Committee considered this to be a matter for the Board of Directors to decide. It would be, indeed, difficult to lay down any rules, in the absence of any practical experience, and it was the wisest course that could have been taken, to leave the matter to the discretion of the Board of Directors.

Two obvious problems arise from this uncertainty:

(1) What rates are to be charged at a given moment to different customers on different kinds of loans?

(2) What principles will be applied to the alteration of these rates from time to time as conditions alter?

A question which at once arises when the problems connected with the Bank scheme are discussed is, whether there will be a uniform "world bank rate", or whether the re-discount rate will vary according to the borrower, according to the currency in which the loan is granted and according to the nature of the security. It is impossible to ascertain what were the intentions of the authors of the scheme upon this question of fundamental importance. The only mention made of interest rates is that the rate on time deposits of

Governments should vary according to the size of the deposit, the period for which it is fixed and the nature of the services rendered. The Bank is entitled to buy bills—including Treasury bills—in any open market at the current rate. The question is what rate it will charge to central banks when they present bills for re-discount from their own portfolio, and what will be the rate charged upon advances made to central banks against security.

It seems obvious that the idea of a "world bank rate" in the sense of a uniform rate to be applied indiscriminately is impracticable. It is impossible to determine a uniform rate irrespective of conditions of security and of the rates of interest prevailing in the countries concerned. If the rate were to be fixed too high it would be prohibitive to some countries, while if it were fixed too low it would unduly encourage some countries to borrow from the Bank. As "risks", all central banks cannot be classed in the same category; the security they provide may also vary; the currency in which they desire to obtain the loan is also an important factor.

When it comes to suggesting a method by which the Bank should differentiate, we soon discover that we are confronted with one of the most complicated problems of modern finance. One solution which suggests itself is to determine the re-discount rate on the basis of the official bank rate of the would-be borrower. Once that principle is accepted, it is necessary to decide whether the re-discount rate should be equal to, higher or lower than, the bank rates of the countries concerned. It is highly questionable, however, whether the adoption of the principle itself is desirable. Central banks requiring the assistance of the Bank would be tempted to

keep their bank rates at an unduly low figure, which
would result in an efflux of foreign funds and would
accentuate the influences that make it necessary to
apply for a credit to the Bank. It would, indeed, amount
to authorising the borrower to fix his own terms, and
would result, in practice, in the repayment of debts owed
to other lenders in order to replace it with cheaper loans
from the Bank. The evil consequences of the method
would become accentuated if the re-discount rate were
to be fixed at a lower figure than the bank rate of the
borrowing countries. The idea itself may appear absurd,
but as, in countries which are the most likely to require
the assistance of the Bank, the bank rate is usually
lower than the market rates, it would not be surprising
to see the claim put forward for a re-discount rate that,
in turn, should be even lower than the bank rate.
Apart from its effect of encouraging the central bank to
keep too low a bank rate, it would also encourage it to
re-discount as much of its portfolio as possible, for the
difference between the bank rate and the re-discount
rate of the Bank for International Settlements would
be the profit of the central bank.

There is more to be said in favour of a re-discount
rate, which, while higher than the bank rates of borrowers, should yet bear a fixed relation to them. The
inducement to keep the bank rate unduly low is less
pronounced than in the case of the two former alternatives, though to some extent it would still be present.
This solution would not be popular, however, among
the countries which are most likely to need the assistance of the Bank, as the bank rate of most of them is
already rather high. The bank rate in any country
is usually determined largely by considerations of the
home money market. In Germany, for instance, first-

class borrowers are usually able to raise funds abroad at a rate below the re-discount rate of their own central banks, while in the domestic market they have to pay a rate above the re-discount rate of the Reichsbank.

The question may also arise how far the currency in which the loan is made should determine the rate. In the case of bills presented for re-discount the currency is usually that of the borrowing country, in which case the rate is largely determined by the rate current in the domestic money market for prime bills, though, in view of the endorsement of the central bank, a lower rate may be acceptable. Very often, however, borrowers would want to raise sterling or dollar or other currency credits, in which case it would be unfair to charge them an interest in accordance with the rates in the domestic market for loans in the domestic currency. As in some cases the leading banks of the country concerned are regular borrowers in foreign markets, the terms on which they can raise funds may be taken for the basis of the calculation of the fair rate of interest.

It appears that the right solution must be to fix the re-discount rate and the rate of advances to meet the particular circumstances of each individual case, taking into consideration the rate at which the Bank itself can borrow in the same currency. This is, undoubtedly, a rather complicated process. It would force the management to follow closely the developments in every money market, and to investigate the position of every central bank. The difficulties in this respect are, however, by no means unsurmountable. After all, commercial banks are confronted with the same problem, and the solution of it has become part of their daily routine. They have no uniform rates for their

customers, and their terms vary according to the
standing of their customer, the nature of the security,
etc. In the discount market the rate quoted by different
houses for fine bank bills may be uniform at a given
moment, but fractional differences above the prime
rate indicate a careful discrimination between names.
The bank rate itself is merely the official minimum,
and central banks may charge higher rates on bills they
want to discourage. For instance, the Bank of France
has raised its re-discount rate for German and other
Central European bills to $\frac{1}{2}$ per cent above the official
minimum rate.

Thus, although it would be simpler for the management of the Bank for International Settlements to
determine their rates of interest by hard and fast
rules rather than to judge each case according to its
merits, there is no need to fear any serious difficulties
in that respect. In any case, it will be desirable for
the Board to leave the discrimination to the management, as far as possible, so as to avoid any introduction of political elements in the determination of
the rates. In order to avoid any ill-feeling, the rates
applied to various central banks should be treated as
strictly confidential.

Hitherto we have been dealing with the factors that
determine the discount rates and rates on advances
charged to various borrowers at a given moment.
There is, in addition, the equally complicated problem
of the general movement of these rates over a period of
time. The Bank will be, naturally, under the influence
of the international trend. An all-round change of
bank rates is bound to affect the lending rates of the
Bank accordingly. The Bank's own position is yet
another factor of supreme importance which ought to

be considered. If the demand for loans is slack, it is justified to lend on lower rates. On the other hand, if there is a strong demand and the Bank is already over-lent, one of the means of discouraging further borrow-ing is to raise the rates. This is one of the reasons why the re-discount rate of the Bank cannot bear any fixed ratio to the bank rates of the borrowing central banks.

Another consideration which will have to be borne in mind is that the Bank will have to endeavour to balance, as far as possible, its assets and its liabilities in any particular currency. For this and other reasons, the Bank may find it desirable to encourage borrowing in one particular currency by charging a compara-tively low rate, and to discourage borrowing in another currency by raising its rates for loans in that currency.

While the discount rates of the Bank will neces-sarily be influenced by conditions in the leading money markets, it would be to underestimate the importance of the institution to suppose that its discount rate policy will consist in the adjustment of its rates to changed circumstances. The Bank will play an active part in influencing tendencies in the international money market with control of the International price-level as one of its most important objectives. The changes in its discount rates should not always be the effect of corresponding changes in general tendencies, but sometimes also their cause. In this sense there may be a question of a "world bank rate", which is, of course, not a single figure as in the case of individual central banks, but a scale of percentages applied in different cases at a given moment. Although the scale itself cannot be published, there is no reason why the extent of an all-round change should not be announced in public.

These are only a few considerations connected with the regulation of the rates of interest to be charged by the Bank. They indicate the extremely complicated nature of the problem. The set of factors affecting the scale of rates to be charged by the Bank are considerably different from those influencing the bank rate in any country. The task of the management of the Bank will be much more difficult than the task of managing any central bank. Whereas the latter have to base their decisions on conditions prevailing in one money market—or, to be more accurate, on the repercussion of domestic and international developments upon the domestic money market—the Bank for International Settlements has to strike a fair balance between the conditions prevailing in every money market. Moreover, the system to be established will not possess the powers of automatic correction of disturbing tendencies which characterise the system of central banking under the gold standard.

The solution of the problems that will arise day after day in connection with fixing rates of interest will require considerable skill and initiative. It is very important, for the success of the Bank, that its management should settle these difficulties in a business-like way, and that they should not take refuge in the red tape of "formulae" drawn up at Board meetings.

CHAPTER XI

INTERNATIONAL GOLD CLEARING

ONE of the objects before the new Bank is to establish
an international gold clearing system, with a view to
reducing unnecessary gold shipments. It was believed
until recently that the preliminary condition of such a
system would be the establishment of an international
central gold reserve. As confidence in international
relations has not been sufficiently established to make
such a scheme possible on a large scale, it must be many
years before the clearing system could be inaugurated
on such basis. Most central banks are anxious to
repatriate the major part of their gold holdings abroad
by the earliest opportunity, and would not contribute
any large amounts of gold towards an international
reserve, even if it were to be held in a neutral country.

The authors of the Bank scheme have, however, hit
upon an ingenious solution to avoid this difficulty.
There is no need for any central gold reserve in order
to enable the participants to establish a clearing
system. The statutes authorise the Bank to accept
from central banks gold in deposit, and to deposit gold
with central banks. As a result, the contribution of
every central bank to the international gold clearing
fund may be kept in deposit with the central bank
itself instead of having to remove it to the headquarters
of the Bank. Thus, if the Bank of England has to

transfer gold to the Bank of France, the Bank for International Settlements reduces the amount earmarked on account of the former and increases the amount earmarked on account of the latter. If before the transaction both institutions had £10,000,000 each earmarked with the Bank, and the Bank had, in turn, £10,000,000 earmarked with each of them, the transfer of £5,000,000 would leave the amount earmarked by the Bank at the Bank of England unchanged, but would reduce to £5,000,000 the amount earmarked by the Bank of England at the Bank for International Settlements; at the same time, the amount earmarked by the Bank at the Bank of France would remain unchanged, while the amount earmarked by the latter at the Bank would increase by £5,000,000. Every year, or every six months, a balance of claims and counterclaims would be struck, and the difference would actually be shipped if necessary.

Technically, the system does not present any particular difficulties. To some extent it has already been practised between central banks. The question is for what purpose the authors of the scheme intend that the system shall be used. There are clearly three possible objects:

(1) To obtain for the Bank and for the participating central banks the monopoly of gold shipments.

(2) To reduce to a minimum the physical displacement of gold across the frontiers.

(3) To avoid superfluous shipments in connection with special transactions.

There has been noticeable during the last few years a tendency on the part of central banks to arrange gold transactions between each other instead of allowing free course to gold arbitrage and confining themselves to the normal devices of monetary policy to influence exchanges so as to initiate or check gold shipments. The comparative frequency of such transactions has led to the assumption that monetary authorities in various countries intend to replace normal commercial shipments by such artificial transactions. Doubtless, central banks are in a position to compete successfully with private arbitrage even without the additional facilities to be provided by the international gold clearing system. As their gold-holding constitutes in any case an idle reserve which earns no interest whether in their vaults or on its way between two centres, there is no need for them to allow anything for loss of interest when calculating the cost of shipment. For this reason they are in a position to undertake gold shipments profitably before any bank or other arbitrageur can see its way to undertake them. The gold points for central banks are, therefore, considerably different from those for other banks.

This, in itself, would not affect the stability of gold points if it were understood that central banks were always supposed to undertake gold shipments whenever exchanges move beyond their special gold points. This, however, is by no means the case. The primary object of gold transactions between central banks is not profit, and they are not likely to undertake gold shipments merely for the sake of the margin of profit, unless there is also another motive which makes their intervention desirable. Consequently, when the exchanges reach their gold points as calculated for central banks, gold may or may not be shipped, according to the convenience of central banks. This state of affairs is bound to create a feeling of uncertainty in the foreign exchange market, as nobody knows whether or not a further depreciation or appreciation of the exchanges would be checked by gold transactions. While the gold points for private arbitrage provide an approximate limit to exchange movements, the gold points for central banks are merely optional limits which may or may not operate in practice.

Possibly the new scheme intends to go further in the same direction and to replace commercial shipments altogether by transfers through international clearing. In that case, the cost of gold movements would disappear altogether, and the central banks would be at liberty to make gold transfers without any loss, at no matter what exchange rate between the gold points. Legally, commercial shipments would remain possible, but the central banks would take care not to allow the exchange to depreciate beyond gold points, and would undertake gold transfers before actual shipments became profitable for private arbitrage. This would be equivalent to the complete loss of the significance of gold points in practice, and the foreign exchange markets and money markets would thereby lose a valuable index. As a result, the influx or efflux of gold through the clearing system would fail to produce the same effect as on the foreign exchange market and the money market as gold movements of the same magnitude undertaken by private arbitrage. These latter usually result in a marked rise or fall, according to the case, in the rates of interest, and tend, therefore, to set the forces in motion which tend to correct the influences responsible for the weakness of the exchange of the exporting country. They also tend to provoke a reaction in the exchange rate itself. On the other hand, if gold transactions are undertaken by central banks through the clearing system, this fact is likely to minimise their effect. Though the contraction of credit resources tends to create monetary stringency, this tendency will not be accentuated by the psychological factor as in the case of arbitrage transactions. If a shipment is made by private arbitrageurs, it is known that so long as the exchange remains at the rate prevailing at the moment of the transaction, several similar transactions will follow. If, on the other hand, a shipment is made by a central bank, it may or may not be followed by other shipments, according to the convenience of central banks. Possibly after an isolated shipment the exchange is allowed to appreciate or depreciate, as the case may be, until it has reached its natural gold point.

The attempt of central banks to monopolise gold shipments would be detrimental to the automatic character of our existing monetary system, which is, after all, one of the principal advantages of the gold standard. It is not likely that the central banks will go so far in this direction—at any rate, not during the early stages of the operation of the new system.

The second possibility is that the principal aim of the clearing system will be to reduce to a minimum the physical movements of gold, without aiming at the acquisition by central banks of a monopoly of gold transactions. The clearing system enables central banks to accept gold delivery at any foreign gold centre, and to pay out gold at any foreign gold centre. If, for instance, the franc were to appreciate beyond gold export point, arbitrageurs need not actually ship gold from London to Paris, but could deposit gold with the Bank of England; the latter would credit the account of the Bank for International Settlements, while that institution, in turn, would credit the account of the Bank of France. Of course, the buying and selling price of gold in case of delivery or demand at a foreign centre would have to take due account of the cost of transport and other expenses, for otherwise the slightest deviation of the exchange from par would result in withdrawals, which is anything but desirable. Thus, gold for the Bank of France would be accepted in London at the rate of, say, 123.88, which is in practice the rate at which gold shipments to France begin. This method is practised already by some central banks which keep permanent external reserves, and the adoption of the new scheme would merely extend it into a general practice.

By such methods it would be possible to reduce to a minimum the physical displacement of gold from one centre to another. The question is whether the change is worth the trouble. When people talk about reducing gold movements they usually have in mind the reduction of the unsettling influence of changes in gold reserves. Neither the limitation of gold movements to central banks nor the reduction of the physical displacement of gold by means of the clearing system would be helpful in that direction. The tendencies which are at present responsible for the fluctuation of gold reserves would continue to operate, and, in spite of the smaller physical movements of funds, they would affect gold reserves to the same extent as the present free movements through normal commercial shipments. All that would happen is that the changes of gold reserve would take place through book-keeping entries instead of through actual shipments.

It may be pointed out that even this development offers great advantages, as it would eliminate the waste of expenses of gold shipments. In reality, however, the amount involved in the actual cost of gold shipments is negligible, and does not, in itself, justify the establishment of a complicated apparatus. After all, the amount spent on gold shipments increases the profits of shipping companies, insurance companies, etc., and is hardly to be counted as a loss to the national income of particular nations.

The only way by which a reduction of the volume of gold movements could prove beneficial is that it should be accompanied by a similar reduction in the fluctuation of gold reserves. This could only be attained by keeping exchange rates in the vicinity of their mint parities, instead of allowing them to fluctuate between their gold points. Though individual central banks may use their foreign exchange reserves to prevent the exchange from reaching its gold points, it is hardly likely that the resources of the Bank for International Settlements would be available to be used systematically for that purpose. It is not the task of the Bank to prevent normal exchange movements, which, though inconvenient, are sometimes useful as shock-absorbers.

It is probable that the primary object of the international clearing system is to eliminate costs of special transactions. Every year a number of shipments are carried out which do not represent profitable exchange transactions, and which involve unnecessary expenses to the central banks in question. To avoid this, the operations will be carried out by means of transfers through the clearing system. To some extent this has already been done in the past. A characteristic example was provided by the triangular gold transactions arranged in May and June 1929 between the Reichsbank, the Federal Reserve Bank of New York, and the Bank of France, and, to a small extent, between the two former and the National Bank of Belgium. The Reichsbank had to sell gold in New York. Instead of shipping gold from Germany, it took over part of the gold earmarked on account of the Bank of France in New York, sold it to the Federal Reserve Bank, and replaced it by means of dispatching gold from its Cologne branch to Paris, which is less expensive than shipments from Bremen or Hamburg to New York. The Bank of France also benefited by the arrangement, as it repatriated free of cost part of its gold held in New York.

The proposed clearing system will make such operations more frequent, but will not interfere with the ordinary commercial transactions to any great extent. Such a change would not be revolutionary, and there is no reason why it should not operate successfully. It is necessary to emphasise, however, that any attempt to interfere with normal gold movements, undertaken to correct credit conditions which have produced the exchange movement responsible for the shipment of gold, would be most undesirable.

CHAPTER XII

WHEN dealing with the political aspects of the Bank for International Settlements scheme, it is necessary to distinguish between its functions in connection with reparations payments and its international banking activities. As far as the former are concerned, the precision with which the Bank's rights and duties are defined in the Young Plan reduces the possibility of political influences acting upon the Bank or through the Bank. As depository of reparations funds, all the Bank has to do is to carry out the letter of the Plan by collecting the amounts transferred by the German Government and by distributing them among the creditor Governments, after having retained the amounts due for the service of the External Loan of 1924 and necessary to pay for its own services. In this respect, it matters little what the political sympathies and antipathies of the Board of Directors are. In the case of the mobilisation of the annuities, there is a somewhat wider scope for political influences, and the same is true of the preventive measures to avert the postponement of transfers. Although the Special Committee to examine the circumstances of the German Government's declaration to suspend transfers may not eliminate politics from its judgement, that committee is not an integral part of the Bank.

The political aspects of the Bank scheme are far more important with regard to the Bank's international banking activities. Assuming that the Bank will develop into an institution of the first magnitude, will be engaged in the distribution of very large credit resources, and will play a prominent part in the regulation of tendencies in the foreign exchange markets, it is by no means indifferent whether or not political considerations may influence its attitude. In this respect there are two principal questions which require answer:

(1) Whether the Bank for International Settlements will come under political influences?

(2) Whether the Bank for International Settlements will exert a political influence of its own?

In the former case the Directors of the Bank are anxious to carry out the political policy dictated to them either by their respective Governments or merely by their patriotic nationalism; while in the latter case they detach themselves from the political influences of their countries of origin, and the Bank will develop a policy of its own, independently of the policy of the countries from which its Directors are delegated.

Should the former be the case, there may be two different results: either the conflicting political interests would paralyse the activities of the Bank, which would then fail to attain its object; or its decisions would take the form of political compromises, without regard to financial considerations.

The first alternative would have a highly detrimental effect upon the Young Plan, as it would practically reduce the Bank to the rôle of a collector and distributor of reparations payments. It is, indeed, difficult to imagine how an institution could fulfil the function of international banker if every application for credit

were to be discussed from a political point of view and
the members of the Board would support or oppose it
according to their political attitude towards the countries concerned. In such circumstances, the country
anxious to obtain credit from the Bank would have
to purchase the support of various Governments by
means of political concessions—a highly undesirable
state of affairs. It is even more likely that an application for credit by one central bank will be favoured by
the representatives of other central banks on a basis
of reciprocity. Each of the leading central banks has
a number of satellites among the smaller central banks,
and it is to be feared that the Directors will form more
or less permanent groups according to the political and
other interests of their countries. Thus, it is by no
means impossible that the Central and Northern European central banks may ally themselves with the Bank
of England, while the Eastern and South-Eastern
European central banks will be in the sphere of the
Bank of France. If one of the members of one group
wants a loan, it may be necessary to promise a loan to
a member of the other group in order to secure a
majority in favour of the transaction. Rival countries
may insist on equal treatment, irrespective of financial
considerations. If Bulgaria gets a loan, Yugoslavia may
threaten to withdraw unless she gets a similar loan;
while Austria may be offended unless she gets credits
simultaneously with Hungary.

Possibly this picture may be too dark, though in
such matters it is safer to err on the side of pessimism.
The fact that the Bank will be in a position to create
fresh credit will certainly encourage excessive demand
for credit, and will make it very difficult for the management to refuse the applications. As was pointed

out in Chapter VIII., the peculiar nature of the Bank enables it to expand credit to a very great extent. Rather than expose themselves to the withdrawal of countries whose interests are not satisfied, or to incessant party strife in Board meetings, the Bank might be tempted to satisfy everybody and thus to go beyond the limits of sound banking.

The other possibility—and here we return to dreams of the future—is that the Directors would detach themselves from the nation which delegated them, and might regard themselves as true citizens of the world whose judgement was independent of the political views of their countries. A situation would then arise for which there is no precedent in history. The Bank would become the arbitrator in conflicts between nations, not merely in financial and economic questions, but possibly even in political questions. Countries bold enough to disobey its ruling would be placed under financial blockade, while obedient countries would be rewarded by financial support. This would be a highly undesirable state of affairs from the point of view of sound banking. It is not properly within the scope of a bank—even if it is an international bank—to interfere with politics. If political conditions in a country are such as to make it unsafe for the banker to invest its money there, then—and only then—he is justified in using discrimination against that country. This practice was adopted by banking interests especially after the war. No loans were granted to countries unless they had a constitutional government. To attempt to influence the outcome of a conflict by means of withholding or granting credit facilities would be, however, an unjustifiable trespass by the Bank in the domain of politics. The ideal state of affairs would be to keep political influences off the Bank, and to keep the Bank out of politics.

There is also a possibility that the Bank would develop into an alliance of central banks to secure their independence against interference on the part of their respective Governments. The statutes show some indication of such a tendency, and it is by no means impossible that the new institution may become the leader of a "hands off central banks" movement. Should this be the case, it would be a point in favour of the Bank, as Government interference with central banks is seldom beneficial to the country concerned. On exceptional occasions central banks are at logger-heads with their Governments for considerations other than those of public interest. For example, the National Bank of Rumania, being controlled by the Liberal party, showed for a time signs of passive resistance against the Government of the National Peasant party. In such cases, however, the Bank will certainly abstain from supporting any central bank.

Very appropriately, the Bank was occasionally re-ferred to as a "financial League of Nations". In fact, an attempt has been made to connect the Bank with the League of Nations; but fortunately the proposal was rejected, on the ground that the association of the Bank with the League would deter American interests from participating in it. The importance of this con-sideration cannot sufficiently be emphasised. Although the State Department is desirous that the Federal Reserve System should keep aloof from the Bank, it has raised no objection to the participation of private banking interests. Should the Bank prove to be suc-cessful, perhaps the American authorities may revise their attitude and co-operate officially with the institution. It would have been a mistake to deter them from doing so by means of associating the Bank with the League, which would have accentuated, at the same time, its political character. Meanwhile, though officially the Federal Reserve System will keep aloof from the Bank, they will nevertheless co-operate with it indirectly, through their contact with the Bank of England. In this respect the situation will remain substantially unchanged, for even up to now the Federal Reserve authorities have preferred to co-operate with European central banks through the Bank of England as an intermediary.

Some political quarters on the Continent are inclined to regard the establishment of the Bank for International Settlements as the first step towards the realisation of their favourite dream of a united front of Europe against the United States. It is hardly necessary to point out the futility of their hopes of using the Bank as a means of separating the two Anglo-Saxon nations from each other. The presence of the representatives of American banking interests on the Board of the Bank is in itself a sufficient guarantee that the institution will not assume an anti-American character. The American banking group, which is entitled to a participation equal to that of any of the principal European central banks, though unofficial, is certainly representative, and is likely to play an active part in the management of the Bank. Its participation disposes of the hopes or fears of a conflict between official United States and the new institution. At the same time, it is only natural that the Bank will, if successful, tend to restore the balance of power in finance which has shifted to a harmful extent towards the United States. In other words, European money markets will be no longer at the mercy of the monetary policy of the Federal Reserve authorities to such extent as during the ten years that followed the armistice. The change is not likely to be viewed with disfavour in Washington and New York, for the responsibility attached to the exceptional position of the Federal Reserve authorities since the war has occasionally proved to be a burden rather than a privilege. The American monetary authorities will be glad to be relieved of that responsibility to some extent, for it will enable them to concentrate on domestic affairs, much to the satisfaction of the Middle West. Indeed, they may themselves feel the need of outside support on occasions when domestic conditions get beyond their control, as was the case during the Wall Street boom of 1928–29.

One of the main points of criticism against the constitution of the Bank is that it secures a predominant interest to the Powers concerned with reparations in problems which have nothing whatever to do with reparations. There is much to justify this criticism, and the only excuse for the arrangement is that it was dictated by practical necessity. The Bank scheme originated through the necessity of creating a reparations bank, and it would be too much to expect that the creditor Governments should admit non-reparations Powers in such an institution on an equal footing. It would have been possible, of course, to come to a compromise whereby the countries not interested in reparations would possess rights proportionate to their financial importance, but would have no vote when matters concerning reparations are at stake. This solution would have been more favourable from the point of view of the Bank's international banking

functions, but would have been less favourable from
the point of view of its reparations functions. One of
the most favourable aspects of the Bank is that it
includes neutral interests, even though they are only
allotted a minority participation. It would have been
unwise to separate the two functions of the Bank into
watertight compartments. As and when the relative
importance of the reparations functions of the Bank
decline in favour of its general international banking
function, then the problem of revising the balance of
power established by the Young Plan will arise. Meanwhile the reduction (as compared with the original plan
in the Young Report) in the influence of the Board of
Directors made by the experts at Baden-Baden and
embodied in the statutes is a step in the right direction.

Both the Young Plan and the statutes have omitted
to deal with the situation that may arise in case of war.
It is essential that the Bank should remain strictly
neutral, and should refrain from granting any credit
to the central bank of a belligerent country. This
should apply even to wars pursued under the auspices
of the League of Nations against disturbers of the
peace. The Bank should, naturally, pay out any deposits it holds on behalf of either party should they
want to withdraw them, and may also accept fresh
deposits or carry out orders on behalf of the central
banks involved. It should not, however, be allowed to
grant any credits unless secured by gold or equivalent
security. This is in accordance with the principles of
prudent banking, as it would be rash to lend to a
country which is engaged in hostilities. Moreover, as
belligerent countries usually suspend the gold standard, that itself would justify the Bank's attitude.

It is necessary to secure the inviolability of the

Bank's gold held abroad, by means of an international Convention or by means of direct treaties between the Bank and foreign Governments. No gold should be deposited with any central bank unless the Government of its country undertakes not to interfere with it under any circumstances, and not to raise any obstacle to its withdrawal even if an embargo is placed on gold exports. As far as the assets held in Switzerland are concerned, they are duly protected by Article 10 of the Charter, in virtue of which "The Bank, its property and assets and all deposits and other funds entrusted to it shall be immune in time of peace and in time of war from any measure such as expropriation, requisition, seizure, confiscation, prohibition or restriction of gold or currency export or import, and any other similar measures." It is highly desirable that the Bank should conclude similar agreements with every country where it intends to hold part of its assets.

CHAPTER XIII

CONCLUSION

THE foregoing chapters have indicated the benefits promised by the scheme of the Bank for International Settlements, and have also underlined the grave dangers involved. The establishment of the Bank constitutes an experiment the result of which, with our present inadequate knowledge, cannot be forecasted with any claim to accuracy. It is not easy to pronounce a preliminary judgement as to whether or not the anticipated advantages of the plan justify Europe in taking the risks involved. The reader, when trying to make up his mind whether to approve or condemn the scheme, has to distinguish between two questions: whether he is for or against the idea of the Bank, and whether or not he approves of the form in which it is put into practice.

There are a great many considerations which may influence one's attitude towards the idea of the Bank. The following are a few of them:

(1) Whether we believe in international institutions.

(2) Whether we consider the present moment as opportune for further progress in the process of internationalisation.

(3) Whether a Bank is the most suitable form for an institution which is to handle reparations.

(4) Whether it is desirable that central banks of

different countries should become partners in a joint enterprise.

(5) Whether it is desirable, or at least permissible, to connect reparations with the movement of co-operation of central banks.

(6) Whether the Bank is likely to become a dangerous rival to existing institutions.

(7) Whether its beneficial results to the community as a whole would be sufficient to outweigh the losses —if any—caused to vested interests.

(8) Whether it is desirable to create an institution which may in time grow to an unexpected and perhaps uncomfortable size.

(9) Whether we believe in the need for credit expansion.

(10) Whether we believe that the credit expansion will be kept within the limits of sound banking.

(11) Whether we believe that the Bank will be too much under political influences.

(12) Whether we are in favour of artificial interference with normal gold movements and exchange movements.

(13) Whether we believe that the Bank will interfere with gold shipments or the Foreign Exchange Market to any great extent.

(14) Whether we believe that the Bank is in a better position than any existing organisation to assist central banks to achieve or maintain the stabilisation of their currencies.

On some of these questions, many people may have strong views which will determine their attitude to the idea of an International Bank. For instance, diehards of all nations, opposed on grounds of principle to international institutions, or ultra-orthodox economists,

opposed to even the smallest dose of credit expansion,
are likely to condemn the idea. Those, however, who
face the fourteen questions with an open mind may
find that, on balance, the probable advantages outweigh the probable disadvantages.

Although existing international institutions—the
League of Nations in the first place—are far from
perfect, it is difficult not to recognise the good work
that they have done, in spite of all their shortcomings.
There is at present a strong tendency, as a reaction
from the war, to strengthen existing international
links and to establish new ones. The International
Bank starts with the tide. As was explained in Chapter
III., the Bank scheme may be regarded as the most
suitable solution of the reparations problem in its
present stage. In view of the benefits of the co-operation between central banks, their closer association
is decidedly advantageous. Although a solution which
links reparations with the movement of co-operation
is far from ideal, there is nothing inherently evil in it.
It is unlikely that the new institution will compete
directly with existing banks, although through its
activities it may divert some business from them. It is
reasonable to expect, however, that the banks will be
compensated for the loss by the benefits of a general
expansion of international financial activities. The
possibility of the institution overreaching itself undoubtedly exists, but the dangers arising from it are
by no means excessive. Credit expansion is to be judged
not as a principle but as a practice: and it is its abuse,
not its use, which is to be feared. As to whether the
management of the Bank will be able to resist political
influences, the outlook is far from reassuring. This
is undoubtedly the most disquieting aspect of the

problem, and it would be self-deception to minimise the extent of the danger.

Most bankers and economists would oppose any interference with the automatic working of gold movements through exchange transactions, and it is unlikely that the Bank will go very far in that direction. It will assist central banks in their task of resisting abnormal exchange fluctuations, but is not likely to attempt to interfere with normal fluctuations within the limits of the gold points.

The question is whether the advantages we shall probably obtain as a result of the Bank's activities make it worth our while to run the grave risk of international credit inflation that may occur as a result of political influences in the management of the Bank. The answer to this question is largely a matter of temperament. Many people are desirous of avoiding any abnormal risk, no matter how much it is outweighed by prospects of ultimate benefit. Such an attitude, if generally adopted, would handicap progress, which is bound to be exceedingly slow unless the world is prepared to take some risk.

It is desirable, however, that, when taking the risk, we should do so with open eyes; that we should be fully aware of its existence and of its possible extent; that we should be in a position to reduce it to a minimum by anticipating the danger.

Experience will show whether or not the Bank plan as elaborated by the Young Committee and by the Organising Committee is the best possible method for obtaining the maximum advantages from the idea, while running the minimum amount of risk. In the course of experience, the shortcomings of the statutes may become evident—in fact, it would be a miracle if statutes drafted in the complete absence of precedents were to satisfy the requirements of practice without amendment. In view of the difficulties that will prevent the making of essential alterations, the interpretations of the statutes by the Board of Directors is of as great importance as the text of the statutes itself. Difficulties and conflicts are likely to arise, especially at the beginning ; but it is to be hoped that they will be solved in a spirit of conciliation, without which even the best statutes, drafted with a super-human foresight of every possible development, could not prevent the Bank from failing to attain its object. It is equally important that the men who guide the Bank should possess sufficient flexibility of personality and of views to allow the Bank to adapt itself to changing conditions.

APPENDIX I

PRELIMINARY ANNOUNCEMENT OF THE BANK SCHEME

The following is the official text of the statement issued on March 9, 1929, by the Committee of Experts in Paris on a "Suggested Plan of a Bank for International Payments":

"As heretofore indicated in the public press, a purely tentative proposal for the organisation of a new International Bank was submitted to the Committee of Experts at a plenary session on March 7.

"Discussion, apart from suggestions, has taken place, and will be reviewed at a plenary session on Monday, March 11.

"Emphasis is laid on the fact that the whole scheme as presented to the Committee of Experts is as yet tentative in character, and, after further examination, is subject to rejection in part or in whole.

"It is obvious that the Committee of Experts, in deciding to explore the possibilities of such a new International Bank, have been impressed with the belief that, in order to achieve a final settlement of Reparations, with which duty the Committee is charged, it will be necessary accordingly to do away with a great part of the temporary war-time machinery that was created to collect Reparations, and for this, if possible, to substitute a permanent peace-time machinery. New machinery may be needed in itself to handle the great new international movement of funds created by the Reparations and War Debts.

"Substitution of financial for political machinery should, it is believed, transfer liquidation of Germany's international obligations from the realm of political discussion to the ordinary forms of business which characterise a state of peace.

"If such an institution were created, its primary function, as in the past, would be to act as trustees, receiving from Germany such annuities as may be arranged and disbursing these among creditor nations.

"As such a link between debtor and creditor, it would facilitate transfers, and it is contemplated that it would finance deliveries in kind; and in important projects coming under the general heading of deliveries in kind, it might, under proper safeguards, finance the residual part of the work.

"It also could co-operate with and act as an essential intermediary between all the existing central and issuing banks in the marketing of such bonds as might be created for the commercialisation of Germany's annuities. It could co-operate with existing banks of issue, and might, if desired, receive both clearing and investment deposits. The large amount of foreign exchange which normally it would hold would fit it for this clearing function, and as a reservoir of foreign exchange it might be of distinct service to existing central banks.

"The outline, as submitted, makes it clear that should this plan meet with financial approval, the institution created would simply avoid competition with existing commercial and investment banking institutions, and would consider it to be a prime necessity to act in close co-operation with existing central banks of issue. In fact, the Bank would co-ordinate and subordinate its activities in any particular country with and to the policies of the existing issuing banks of that country.

"The new Bank would be in no sense a super-bank to exercise a dominating influence over existing institutions. The authors of the suggestion believe that the operations of the new institution would tend to increase and strengthen the co-operation that already has been developed between central banks, and which has been of such marked service during the past several years in restoring the gold standard throughout the world and in other ways stabilising financial conditions. It would supplement rather than duplicate existing institutions, and it would assist rather than direct.

"As to management, the scheme makes it clear that the Bank, if organised, must be non-political, must be international, and free from any dominating financial relationships.

"Upon the directorate should sit only men of experience and financial repute. As supplementary to the directorate, advisory committees are suggested, composed in such manner as might be necessary to secure sound opinion on the problems to be dealt with.

"The offices of the Bank would probably be in one of the smaller countries where a suitable legal status and freedom from taxation may be obtained.

"It is believed that the operations of the Bank would be of advantage equally to the debtor and creditor nations. With the establishment of such financial machinery, Germany would stand on her own feet financially, would have the responsibility of obtaining her own credit, and would be dealing on a business basis with an international financial institution operated on sound business principles.

"In addition to bringing these advantages, the Bank would be in a position to aid the Reichsbank and other central banks in the work of obtaining the stability of their exchanges, and so to assist in obtaining steady business conditions generally.

"To creditor nations it would be valuable as facilitating the uninterrupted flow of annuities and furnishing readier facilities for the ultimate commercialisation of the German Debt.

"The creditor nations would also participate in the profits that the Bank might reasonably be expected to earn.

"The new Bank might serve to fill in possible gaps that now exist in the world's banking organisations, and particularly such a gap as may have resulted from the new situation created by the Reparations and Debt Settlements.

"The discussions of the Committee next week are intended to clarify the project and to bring the Committee to a determination as to whether to proceed further with this plan or whether to postpone further consideration of it."

APPENDIX II

EXTRACTS FROM THE REPORT OF THE COMMITTEE OF EXPERTS ON REPARATIONS

The following is the text of those parts of the Young Report and its Annexes which deal with the Bank for International Settlements:

EXTRACT FROM PART 5 (COURSE OF THE PROCEEDINGS)

THE arrangements that have been in force under the Dawes Scheme for liquidating a part of the annuity by means of deliveries in kind required consideration from two points of view: (*a*) the substitution for the existing methods of a more elastic machinery which, as the Dawes Committee recommended, should be non-political; and (*b*) the gradual termination of the system at the earliest moment consistent with existing relationships and with the interests of Germany, whose economic life has been during the past few years gradually adapted to them, and who would feel herself prejudiced in an economic sense by their too sudden termination.

The enquiries upon these subjects were found to be converging upon one central point, viz., the nature of the authority which should act as the chief medium for discharging the various functions under a new plan.

In the exploration of the problem of substituting authority of an external, financial and non-political character for the present machinery and controls of the Dawes Plan (viz., the administration of the Agent-General and of the various Commissioners in Berlin, and those functions of the Reparation Commission which were involved), they immediately met with the necessity for a Trustee to whom the payments in foreign currencies and Reichsmarks should be made by Germany, and by whom the distribution to the appropriate recipients should be managed.

In the second place, the problems of mobilisation and commercialisation demanded a common centre of action and authority for the purpose of co-ordinating and controlling the arrangements, and there were obvious advantages in such an authority being of a continuous or permanent character.

In the third place, the continued existence of Deliveries in Kind necessitated special machinery of direction and control, at any rate for a period of years.

They had already considered the desirability of an advisory committee which could take any necessary action in connection with the declaration of a postponement on the postponable part of the annuity. A permanent central authority might include among its functions the convening of such an advisory body, international in character and existing as a constituent part of this central authority, to consider the situation which had brought about the necessity for a postponement, or the situation which a postponement itself created.

Again, the possibility that, either exceptionally or regularly as part of the plan, obligations would be discharged in marks within Germany necessitated a financial authority to arrange for the disposition of such funds or assets in the interests of the Creditors, by arrangement with the Reichsbank or other German authority.

Moreover, in so far as the task of transferring the payments into foreign currencies involved, besides a restriction of imports, an extension of German export trade, we envisaged the possibility of a financial institution that should be prepared to promote the increase of world trade by financing projects, particularly in undeveloped countries, which might otherwise not be attempted through the ordinary existing channels.

These several considerations led the Committee to the elaboration of a plan for a Bank for International Settlements, which should, in its various functions, meet all these points. The outline of this scheme is given in Section 6 and Annex I.

6.—BANK FOR INTERNATIONAL SETTLEMENTS

A.—*General Reasons for the Constitution of an Institution with Banking Functions*

A general plan for a complete and final settlement of the reparation problem, being primarily financial in character, involves the performance of certain banking functions at one or more points in the sequence between the initial payment of the annuities and the final distribution of the funds. A banking institution designed to meet these requirements justifies and makes logical the liquidation of all political controls, and provides instead machinery essentially commercial and financial in character, which carries with it all the support and, at the same time, all the responsibilities that economic engagements imply. The process of removing the reparation problem from the political to the financial sphere, which was begun in the Dawes Plan, will thus be carried a step further.

In general terms, the institution will take over such functions of the existing agencies as it may be necessary to continue and will perform the whole work of external administration, such as the receipt and distribution of payments and the commercialisation of those parts of the annuities which are susceptible of being commercialised.

The operations of the institution will be assimilated to ordinary commercial and financial practice. Its organisation will be outside the field of political influences, and its powers and facilities will be sufficiently broad to enable it to deal freely and promptly with the problems involved in the settlement of Germany's obligations. The institution will be equipped with machinery which will provide an elastic element between the payments to be made by Germany and their realisation. In consequence, the Creditors will have further assurance that the effects of economic changes on the flow of payments will be minimised, and Germany for her part will have the possibility of assistance during temporarily unfavourable conditions.

It is obviously desirable, in the interest of obtaining results with the greatest efficiency, not to limit unduly the functions of the institution. The character of the annuities, and the magnitude of the payments to be transferred over the exchanges, provide at once the opportunity and the need for supplementing with additional facilities the existing machinery for carrying on international settlements, and within limitations of the sound use of credit to contribute to the stability of international finance and the growth of world trade. We consider that by judicious non-competitive financial development the Bank should prove a useful instrument for opening up new fields of commerce, of supply and of demand; and will thus help to solve Germany's special problem, without encroaching on the activities of existing institutions.

In designing the Plan for the Bank for International Settlements, which is given in outline in Annex I., we were therefore mindful of the fact that these new facilities should not supplant but should augment and perfect existing arrangements for carrying through international settlements. The Bank will have (a) as its essential or obligatory functions those which are inherent in the receipt, management and distribution of the annuities; and (b) as its auxiliary or permissive functions those which evolve more indirectly from the character of the annuities. There is no hard-and-fast line between the two sets of functions, because the first lead naturally into second.

B.—*Organisation of the Bank*

In view of the part which the Bank will have to play in the general interest, it is advisable to place the control of its management in the hands of the central banks, since these are the organisations responsible in each market for the convertibility of the national currencies and the control of credit.

At the time of the Bank's constitution the capital will be geographically distributed in such a way as to associate in the Bank's working and in its development all the countries interested in the reparation settlement and all the financial markets which may subscribe to the Bank's issues.

Provision is made for the utilisation of the net profits of the Bank, due allowance being made for the payment of cumulative dividends on the capital stock, to create suitable reserve funds. Provision is also made, in case Governments or central banks make long-term deposits with the Bank, whereby they shall share proportionately in the remainder of the profits, after the requirements on account of dividends and the reserve funds have been covered.

Inasmuch as its international basis is an essential feature which distinguishes the institution from all others, it has no single fiscal allegiance, and it is desirable that in its movements in the various national markets it should not be hampered or restricted by considerations of relative fiscal burdens. It is therefore recommended that the Governments of the countries concerned enter into a Convention for the avoidance of double and triple taxation of the Bank along the following lines:

> (*a*) The funds and investments of the Bank to be freed from national taxation at the point where they derive interest, income and profit;
>
> (*b*) all individuals and corporations receiving profit, interest or income from the Bank to be fully liable thereon to such taxation as such individuals and corporations would attract if the profit, interest or income were derived from any other source.

(1) *Capital.*—On the formation of the Bank its authorised capital will be in the equivalent of $100,000,000. The entire amount will be issued, but only 25 per cent of each share shall be called up, until the Board of Directors decides on a further call. The allocation of shares by countries is provided for in Section II. of Annex I. The shares will carry no voting rights; but voting rights corresponding to the number of shares first issued in each country will be exercised by the central bank of that country in general meetings attended by representatives of those banks, taking the place of general meetings of shareholders.

(2) *Administration.*—The entire administrative control of the Bank will be vested in the Board of Directors. The functions of a Director of the Bank are incompatible with those involving national political responsibilities, and the statutes of the Bank

will make the necessary provision in order to avoid such conflict of functions. All the Directors and candidates shall be ordinarily resident in Europe, or shall be in a position to give regular attendance at meetings of the Board.

The Governor of the central bank of each of the seven countries to which members of the present Experts' Committee belong, or his nominee, will be entitled to be a Director of the Bank *ex officio*. Each of these Governors may also appoint one Director, being a national of his country and representative either of finance or of industry or commerce. During the period of the German annuities the Governor of the Bank of France and the President of the Reichsbank may each appoint, if they so desire, one additional Director of his own nationality, being a representative of industry or commerce. These fourteen (or, as the case may, sixteen) Directors will elect not more than nine additional Directors from lists furnished by, and which may include, the Governors of central banks in other participating countries.

If in the process of organising the Bank or in the performance of its functions after establishment, it is found that the central bank of any country or its Governor is unable to act officially or unofficially in exercising the functions, authorities or privileges accorded to central banks under the Plan, or refrains from doing so, alternative arrangements not inconsistent with the laws of that country will be made. These alternative arrangements are outlined in Section XII. of Annex I.

(3) *Distribution of Profits.*—The profits shall be divided in accordance with the provisions contained in Annex I.

C.—*General Observations on the Bank*

The foregoing outline of the functions and organisation of the Bank for International Settlements, together with the fuller presentation of the Bank Plan in Annex I., largely speaks for itself. It remains, however, to point out certain advantages which the Bank offers as against the existing Reparation procedure, and which advantages accrue both to Germany and to the creditor countries, because the Bank in putting the payments on a business basis makes their receipts the more certain, and facilitates their movement. The new facilities introduced by the Bank are in addition to the provisions given elsewhere in the Plan whereby Germany is entitled to declare a postponement of transfer. They are rather in the nature of forestalling circumstances which might of themselves lead to a transfer postponement. These measures of prevention are of two general sorts: first, the Bank may employ its power of giving credit to arrange temporary assistance in transferring the annuities; second, the Bank will be in a position, in agreement with the Reichsbank, to invest in Germany Reichsmarks currently accruing to its account at the Reichsbank. This measure to the extent to which it may be utilised will return to the German economy a portion of the annuity, and through the Bank's credit mechanism provide the foreign exchange with which to pay the current allotments to the creditors on account of the annuity. The application of either or both of these measures is prompt and decisive, and they operate in advance of the time when difficulties present themselves rather than afterwards, and serve to ease any strain until such time as the discount rate and other corrective measures have had opportunity to exert themselves.

It is not to be assumed that these two measures should be reserved for emergency use. The use of the Bank's credit by central banks within moderate limits, and over short periods, may in time become a normal function scarcely different in its exercise from the use of central bank credit by banks and bankers. All central banks, for ordinary exchange operations or for other purposes, would frequently find it advantageous to make use of the facility. The second measure, that of investing within Germany some portion of the annuity receipts, should also find its uses in normal times. Both measures are necessarily limited by the funds which the Bank will have at its disposal and by the requirement that it maintains its liquidity at all times.

These are instances of the Bank's utility to Germany. They also illustrate the flexibility which the Bank's facilities give to the handling of the disbursements to the creditors. Further instances of joint benefit may be briefly indicated. The Bank will be able to give short-term and intermediate credit to purchasers of deliveries in kind, notably for the construction of public works on delivery-in-kind account. Intermediate credit operations need not be restricted, however, to any one country or to the purchase of any one country's goods. On the contrary, it would be desirable to broaden such operations in the interest of world trade to the extent that the Directors of the Bank approve. As a stabilising factor in the foreign exchanges its advantages are obvious; and if in due time the arrangements provided for an international settlement fund are put into effective operation, the Bank should go far to eliminate the costs and risks now incurred in the shipping and re-shipping of gold.

The Bank excludes from its procedure all political influences, and business principles and practice intervene to facilitate the settlement of Germany's obligations without in any way qualifying her independent and sole responsibility. The Office for Reparation Payments and its associated organisations in Berlin will be retired, and the Reparation Commission's relations with Germany will be terminated. Germany will assume the responsibility for raising and transferring the annuities, and the Bank takes over the work of their receipt and disbursement.

As already stated, the Bank is so designed as not to interfere with the functions performed by existing institutions, but it is to create for itself supplementary functions in a special field of its own. To this end every care should be exercised in the organisation and administration of the institution.

In the natural course of development, it is to be expected that the Bank will in time become an organisation, not simply, or even predominantly, concerned with the handling of reparations, but also with furnishing to the world of international commerce and finance important facilities hitherto lacking. Especially it is to be hoped that it will become an increasingly close and valuable link in the co-operation of Central Banking institutions generally—a co-operation essential to the continuing stability of the world's credit structure.

K

EXTRACTS FROM PART 8 (ANNUITIES)

8 (e) MEASURES OF SAFEGUARD

The essence of the additional margin of safety given to a part of the annuities lies in the power to postpone transfer. We are recommending, in order to protect Germany against the possible consequence of a comparatively short period of depression, which might, for internal or external reasons, put such a severe strain on the exchanges as would make the process of transfer abroad dangerous, that the German Government should have the right, on giving 90 days' notice, to postpone transfers for a period not exceeding two years under conditions set out in Annex IV. During the period of postponement, the liability of the German Government with regard to the sums affected would in the first instance be limited to payments in Reichsmarks to the account at the Reichsbank of the Bank for International Settlements; under certain conditions, part of this payment may also be withheld.

Upon the declaration of any postponement the Bank for International Settlement shall convene the Special Advisory Committee. At any other time, when the German Government declare to the Creditor Governments and to the Bank for International Settlements that they have come to the conclusion in good faith that Germany's exchange and economic life may be seriously endangered by the transfer in part or in full of the postponable portion of the annuities, the Committee shall also be convened.

Upon being convened, the Special Advisory Committee shall forthwith consider the circumstances and conditions which have led up to the necessity for postponement, or have created a situation in which Germany considers that her exchange and economic life may be seriously endangered by further transfers of the postponable portion of the annuity, and make a full investigation of Germany's position in regard to her obligations under this Plan.

In their report to the Governments and to the Bank, having (in case of a postponement of transfer) satisfied themselves that the German authorities have used every effort in their power to fulfil their obligations, they shall indicate for consideration by the Governments and the Bank what in their opinion are the measures that should be taken in regard to the application of the present Plan.

It shall further be the duty of the Bank during a postponement of transfer to direct, in conjunction with the Reichsbank, the employment of the Reichsmarks paid to its account at the Reichsbank by the German Government. (See Section VI. of Annex I. to this Report.)

The following paragraphs sketch the organisation of the Special Advisory Committee of the Bank for International Settlements, referred to in the preceding paragraphs:

1. The Committee shall act in a purely consultative capacity. Its findings shall have no effective force unless confirmed and accepted by the Bank as Trustee of the Creditors, and if necessary by the Governments concerned.

2. The Committee shall play no part in connection with the unconditional annuity accepted by Germany and referred to in the Plan as the "unconditional annuity".

3. The Committee shall be convened by the Bank according to the rules of its own constitution when notice shall be received from the German Government. It shall not be required to meet at any other time.

4. The Committee shall consist of seven ordinary and four co-opted Members. The ordinary Members shall be nominated one by each of the following:

The Governors of:
    The Reichsbank,
    The Banque de France,
    The Bank of England,
    The Banque Nationale de Belgique,
    The Banca d' Italia,
    The Bank of Japan,
    A Federal Reserve Bank of the United States or some
        other agreed American financial institution;

in the last two cases, such nominee being ordinarily resident in Europe or in a position to give prompt attendance on a meeting of the Committee being called. These nominees of the Governors of the Banks shall not be officially connected with the banking institutions in question nor with the Government departments of their respective countries. After being summoned they may, if they so desire, co-opt not more than four additional members with the intent that special aspects, whether in finance, exchange, industry, etc., of the particular situation in question shall be represented. During the course of the proceedings and until the report is made, the co-opted members shall be equal in all other respects to the ordinary members, but they shall thereafter be discharged from office.

5. The Committee may proceed by way of hearing evidence or asking for documents, as it may desire, but the President of the Reichsbank and/or any other person nominated by the German Government may appear before or submit to the Committee the reasons for which a postponement has been declared or measures are desirable as indicated above.

The Committee shall neither grant nor refuse a postponement. After making enquiry, it shall report to the Governments and the Bank as indicated above.

6. Unless otherwise arranged by consent the expenses of the Special Advisory Committee shall be borne by the German Government.

The Bank for International Settlements shall manage the disbursements on deliveries in kind account, and in making distributions of cash to the Creditor countries shall have due regard for those portions of the annuity which are restricted to payments for deliveries in kind.

10.—COMMERCIALISATION AND MOBILISATION

Having recommended the creation of the Bank for International Settlements in order to provide machinery for the removal of the Reparation obligation from the political to the financial sphere, we have further considered what procedure is necessary in order to assimilate this obligation as closely as possible to an ordinary commercial obligation ("commercial-isation").

Further, certain Governments are known to attach particular importance to the possibility of raising money by the issue to the public of Bonds representing the capitalisation of the unconditional portion of the Annuity ("mobilisation").

It is of course not within our power to advise as to the time at which such issues can be made with advantage, or as to the terms and conditions on which issues should be made. The arrangements to be made would no doubt vary according as, for example, an issue is to be made for cash in the general interest of all the Creditor Governments, or an internal issue is to be made in one single country by way of conversion of Government Debt. It will be the province of the Bank itself to advise upon such matters; but we have thought it necessary to advise a framework within which these operations may take place.

This framework is given in Annex III. It provides first that the Annuities themselves shall be represented by a German Government certificate of indebtedness deposited with the Bank, similar to those in use in ordinary commercial practice (a proper distinction being made in the coupons between the conditional and unconditional portions of the Annuity). The provisions regarding security are given in the Annex and the conditions in which mobilisable Bonds should be created and issued are defined.

One of the most important provisions of this scheme is that annuity moneys should be distributed by the Bank in strict proportion to the rights of each party—whether Government or bondholder.

EXTRACTS FROM PART 11 (THE NEW PLAN CONTRASTED WITH THE DAWES PLAN)

(7) *Financial Organisation*

The organisation and machinery of the Dawes Plan were based on the conviction that it must find its proper guarantee in the interests of all parties to carry it out in good faith. In aiming as it did at the transference of the Reparation payments from the political to the economic and business sphere, it presumed constant co-operation of debtor and creditors alike. The new system goes further along the same road, replacing the collaboration of separate administrative and governmental organisation by common work in a purely financial institution, in the management of which Germany is to have an appropriate part. The present administrative organisations cannot have all the elasticity necessary for banking transactions of the magnitude of the payment and transfer of the annuities; but the new Bank in close association with the banks of issue and with the banking facilities at its command will have all the necessary means of effecting these operations without disturbance to the German economy or to the economy of other countries. In addition it will be in a position to open up to trade new possibilities of development. The operations which it is to undertake cannot be disturbed or hampered without irreparable damage to the credit of the countries concerned. This assurance should make it possible to limit the guarantees established under the present system for the protection of the rights of the creditors, to the minimum required for the prompt and facile commercialisation of the mobilisable part of the annuity.

ANNEX I

SUGGESTED OUTLINE FOR THE ORGANISATION OF THE BANK FOR INTERNATIONAL SETTLEMENTS

In Section III. of the following outline, provision is made for an Organisation Committee, which will have the duty of putting the Bank project into effect. This outline has been drawn up for the benefit of the Organisation Committee, which will have power generally to modify its provisions or to make substitutions for any or all of them; provided always that such modifications or substitutions shall not be inconsistent with the essential functions of the Bank with respect to the Experts' Plan as a whole.

I.—Purpose, Name and Location

The Bank organised under this Plan shall be known as the "Bank for International Settlements".

The purpose of the Bank is to provide additional facilities for the international movement of funds, and to afford a ready instrument for promoting international financial relations. In connection with the German reparation annuities, it shall perform as trustee for the creditor countries the entire work of external administration of this Plan, shall act as the agency for the receipt and distribution of funds, and shall supervise and assist in the commercialisation and mobilisation of certain portions of the annuities.

It shall be located in a financial centre hereafter to be designated. In selecting the country of incorporation, due consideration shall be given to obtaining powers sufficiently broad to enable it to perform its functions with requisite freedom and with suitable immunities from taxation.

II.—Share Capital

The authorised capital of the Bank may be expressed in the currency of the country of domicile, and shall amount to the round equivalent of $100,000,000. Upon the formation of the Bank the whole authorised capital shall be issued, but only 25 per cent of each share shall be then paid in. The Board of Directors of the Bank shall have power to call for the payment of further instalments; it shall also have the power to authorise an increase or a reduction in the total capital stock of the Bank.

In each country in which the shares of the Bank may be offered for sale, the shares shall be issued through the central bank of that country or other agency to which the central bank offers no objection. In the seven countries to which members of the present Committee belong, issues or allocations of shares shall always be made in equal amounts. The central banks of these countries, or banking groups not objected to by them, shall guarantee the subscription of the whole of the first issue in the round equivalent of $100,000,000; but they may agree with central banks or groups in other countries (particularly those interested in reparations) that an amount of the first issue not exceeding the round equivalent of $4,000,000 for each, and not exceeding the round equivalent of $44,000,000 in all, may be issued in other countries.

In the event of an increase in the authorised capital and a further issue of shares, the distribution among countries shall be decided by a two-thirds majority of the Directors of the Bank on the above principles. In particular, the percentage of the total shares issued in the seven countries first mentioned above shall not fall below 55.

Apart from countries interested in reparations, only countries which have, at the time an offering of shares is made, a currency stabilised on a gold or gold exchange basis may participate.

The shares may be expressed in the currency of the country in which the Bank is domiciled, and shall state the amount of the share at the gold mint parity of the currency of the country in which they are issued; they shall be registered and continue to be registered, but may be freely negotiated. Transfers of the shares after issue shall not affect the voting power reserved to the central banks as described below. Payments to the shareholders on account of dividends or at the liquidation of the Bank shall be made in the currency of the country of domicile.

The shares shall carry no voting rights; but voting rights corresponding to the number of shares originally issued in each country shall be exercised by the central bank of that country in the general meetings of the Bank (taking the place of the general meetings of shareholders), which the representatives of the participating central banks will attend.

The shares shall be entitled to participate in the profits of the Bank as indicated in the section "Distribution of Profits".

III.—Organisation Committee

For the purpose of taking the preliminary steps for putting the Bank project into effect a temporary Committee shall be created, which will be known as the "Organisation Committee".

This Committee shall be appointed by the Governors of the central banks of the seven countries to which members of the present Committee belong. The Governor of each of these seven central banks shall be entitled to designate two members of the Organisation Committee, with due regard for the necessity of including in its membership persons versed in banking, the issue of bonds and the work of the present Committee of Experts. If for any reason the Governor of any of these central banks shall be unable officially or unofficially to designate members of the Organisation Committee, or refrains from doing so, the Governors of the remaining central banks shall invite two fellow-nationals of the Governor not participating to act as members of the Committee. The members thus selected shall have in all respects an equal vote in the work of the Committee with the members otherwise chosen. The decisions of the Organisation Committee shall be taken by a three-quarters vote.

As an essential part of its work the Organisation Committee shall proceed with drawing up a charter for the Bank, which shall be consistent with the provisions of the Plan, and shall take such steps as may be necessary to ensure its timely granting or enactment by appropriate public authorities.

The Organisation Committee shall, until such time as the Board of Directors of the Bank is appointed and takes office, proceed with the physical organisation of the Bank. It shall arrange, in accordance with the procedure prescribed in Section II., for the subscription of the capital stock, and in accordance with the procedure prescribed in Section IV., for the appointment of the Board of Directors. It shall call the first meeting of the Board of Directors, and designate the temporary Chairman to preside at that meeting pending the election of the regular Chairman. It shall draw up the statutes for regulating the administration of the Bank and submit them to the Board of Directors for consideration. These statutes shall make provision for such matters as are usual in banking organisation, and in particular provide for the following:

(1) The qualifications for membership on the Board of Directors.

(2) The nature and duties of the permanent committees of the Board of Directors, including the Executive Committee.

(3) The administrative departments to be created within the Bank.

(4) The time and place of the meetings of the Board of Directors and of the Executive Committee.

(5) The form to be used for the convocation of the General Meeting, as well as the conditions and the methods for exercising voting rights on the part of representatives of central banks.

(6) The form of trust certificates which the Bank shall issue to the creditor Governments under the Plan.

(7) Provisions with regard to liquidation of the Bank.

The Organisation Committee shall co-operate with the organisation committees provided for in this Plan.

IV.—DIRECTORATE AND MANAGEMENT

The entire administrative control of the Bank shall be vested in the Board of Directors, whose duty it shall be to supervise and direct the operations of the Bank and in general so to act as to carry out those purposes of the Plan committed to the administration of the Bank. In particular, the Board of Directors:

(1) Shall have the right to adopt, modify, limit or extend the statutes of the Bank in such a manner as shall not be inconsistent with the provisions of the Plan.

(2) Shall have the power generally to modify the provisions contained in the outline of the Bank's organisation or to make substitutions for any or all of them, provided always that such modifications or substitutions shall not be inconsistent with the essential functions of the Bank with respect to the Experts' Plan as a whole and with its existing engagements.

(3) Shall appoint the chief executive officer of the Bank, and fix his remuneration.

(4) May appoint an Executive Committee and delegate

such powers to it as may be provided for in the statutes of the Bank.

(5) May appoint advisory committees to deal with any questions upon which information or advice is desired.

The functions of a Director are incompatible with those involving national political responsibilities. The statutes of the Bank shall make the necessary provision in order to avoid such conflict of functions. All the Directors shall be ordinarily resident in Europe or shall be in a position to give regular attendance at meetings of the Board.

The Board of Directors shall be made up in the following manner:

(1) The Governor (or, as the case may be, the chief executive officer) of the central bank of each of the seven countries to which members of the present Committee belong, or his nominee, shall be a Director of the Bank *ex officio*. Each of these Governors shall also appoint one Director, being a national of his country and representative either of finance or of industry or commerce. In case the Governor or any central bank shall be unable to act either officially or unofficially according to the provisions of this paragraph, or refrains from doing so, action shall then be taken in accordance with the alternative procedure given in Section XII. of this outline.

(2) During the period of the German annuities the Governor of the Bank of France and the President of the Reichsbank may each appoint, if they so desire, one additional Director of his own nationality, being a representative of industry or commerce.

(3) The Governor of the central bank of each of the other countries participating in the share ownership of the Bank as provided in Section II. of this outline, shall furnish a list of four candidates of his own nationality for directorships. Two of the candidates on each list shall be representative of finance and the other two of industry or commerce. The Governors in question may themselves be included in this list. From these lists the fourteen or sixteen Directors mentioned

in paragraphs (1) and (2) above shall elect not more than nine other Directors.

(4) From those first appointed, four groups of five Directors shall be chosen by lot; their terms respectively shall end at the close of each of the first, second, third and fourth years from the establishment of the Bank. Subject to this, the term of office of the Directors shall be five years, but they may be reappointed.

(5) In case of vacancy in a position on the Board of Directors arising from death, resignation or other causes, the vacancy shall be filled in the same manner as prescribed for original appointments. If a vacancy occurs before the expiration of a term, it shall be filled for the remainder of the term only.

The Directors shall elect a Chairman annually from among their own number. The Chairman's duties shall be to preside at meetings of the Board of Directors. At the first meeting, until the Chairman shall have been elected, a member of the Board selected for the purpose by the Organisation Committee shall act as Chairman.

The ordinary decisions of the Board, including those involving elections, shall be made by a simple majority vote. In case of an even division the Chairman shall have a deciding vote. For decisions involving the adoption or amendment of statutes of the Bank, modifications or substitutions in the present project for the organisation of the Bank, the distribution among countries of additional issues of stock in the Bank, or other matters for which the statutes of the Bank make appropriate provision, a two-thirds majority shall be required. Should a member not be able to attend a meeting of the Board, it will always be open to him to empower one of his colleagues, by registered letter or by telegram, to vote for him and on his behalf.

If decisions of the Board are disputed on the ground that they are inconsistent with the provisions or intent of the Plan, recourse may be had to arbitration under the procedures laid down in Part 8 of the Plan.

The chief executive officer of the Bank shall select the officers and heads of the departments of the Bank. For the latter the appointments shall be subject to the approval of the Board of Directors.

V.—Deposits

The Bank, in carrying out its functions with respect to the facilitation of international settlements or in connection with the German annuities, shall have the right to receive deposits of a nature consistent therewith. The Board of Directors, or, as it may decide, the Executive Committee, shall consider applications to open deposit accounts, with authority to determine whether such applications come within the scope of the Bank's functions. Deposits shall be received in only those currencies which satisfy in the opinion of the Board of Directors the practical requirements of the gold or gold-exchange standard.

Any classification of deposits which the Board of Directors may set up shall include:

(1) Deposits on annuity account. These deposits the Bank receives in its capacity as Trustee for the creditor Governments. They shall be managed according to the procedure given in Section VIII. of this outline.

(2) Deposits from central banks. These may be either current account deposits or investment account deposits.

(3) Deposits on clearing account. The Bank shall have the right, subject to such terms and conditions as the Board of Directors may set down, to accept deposits from central banks for the purpose of establishing and maintaining a fund for settling accounts among them. Such deposits may take the form of gold deliveries at the counters of the Bank or of gold held for its account under earmark by any central bank participating in the fund for clearing accounts. The terms under which central banks may enter the clearing system, the rules and regulations for its operation, and the rates of exchange at which gold is to be accepted as deposits in the clearing fund or to be withdrawn from it, shall be determined by the Board of Directors of the Bank.

(4) Deposits originating in the exercise of the Bank's

functions in connection with the German annuities, and tending to facilitate such functions. No such account shall be opened without the assent of the central bank of the country of which the prospective depositor is a national. If the Governor of the central bank in question (or his nominee) is present and voting at the time the Board of Directors (or the Executive Committee) of the Bank authorises the opening of the account, his favourable vote shall be taken as giving the required assent.

(5) Deposits constituting guarantee funds, as provided in Annex VIII. and relative to the mobilisation of the unconditional annuity. The interest and the share in the profits which will apply to these deposits are provided for in Annex VIII. and in the section on Profits in this outline.

(6) Special deposit of the German Government. During the first 37 years the German Government shall maintain at the Bank a non-interest-bearing deposit equivalent to 50 per cent of the average deposit remaining in the Annuity Trust Account, as described in Section VIII. of this outline. This German Government deposit will not exceed 100 million Reichsmarks.

The Bank shall have the right to pay interest on deposits, but only on deposits not susceptible of withdrawal until at least one month from the time of deposit. The rate of interest to be paid will be determined by the Board of Directors, or, as the case may be, by the Executive Committee. In allowing interest on deposits, the Board of Directors shall give due consideration to the value of the services performed for the depositor and the size of the depositor's balance.

VI.—Loans, Discounts and Investments

The Board of Directors shall determine the nature of the operations to be undertaken by the Bank. Such operations shall be consistent with the policies of the central banks of the countries concerned. The Bank may in particular have the right (a) to deal directly with central banks, or (b) to deal through central banks which have agreed to act as its agent and correspondent, or (c) to deal with banks, bankers, corporations and individuals of any country in performing any authorised function provided the central bank of that country does not enter objection. Whenever any proposed credit operation affecting any particular market comes up for decision, the favourable vote of the Governor of the central bank concerned (or his nominee if the Governor is not present), sitting as a member of the Board of Directors or the Executive Committee, shall be taken as giving the assent of his central bank. If he declines to give his assent, the proposed credit operation shall not be undertaken in his market.

Thus the Bank may perform such functions as the following:

(1) To buy and to sell gold coin and bullion, to earmark gold for the account of central banks, and to make advances to central banks on gold as security.

(2) To buy and to sell for its own account, either with or without its endorsement, bills of exchange and other short-term obligations of prime liquidity, including cheques drawn or endorsed by central banks or in respect of which three obligees are responsible.

(3) To open and maintain deposit accounts with central banks.

(4) To re-discount for central banks bills taken from their portfolios, to make loans to them on the security of such bills, or to make advances to them against the pledge of other securities up to such amounts and for such periods as may be approved by the Board of Directors.

(5) To buy and to sell for its own account intermediate or long-terms securities (other than shares) of a character approved by the Board of Directors. Its holdings of such securities at any one time shall not exceed the total of its paid-in capital and reserve funds.

(6) To invest in Germany, with the assent of the Reichs-bank, Reichsmark funds standing to the credit of the Bank at the Reichsbank which are not transferable owing to a declaration of transfer postponement. The Bank may realise

upon any such investments at its discretion unless at the time the investment was agreed to by the Reichsbank some stipulation or arrangement affecting the possible sale was made a condition of such agreement. The income from any such investments and the proceeds of such investments if sold, shall be deposited to the credit of the Bank at the Reichsbank. Such funds may be held as deposits under the conditions set out in Annex IV. of the Plan or be reinvested consistently with the provisions of that Annex.

If in the opinion of the Board of Directors of the Bank, counter-obligations issued against its investments in Germany as collateral can be advantageously sold on non-German markets, their net proceeds shall be distributed to the creditor countries in such proportions and under the same conditions as would have applied in the case of normal transfer. The accounts of the creditor Powers shall be charged with the Reichsmark cost of the securities alienated or pledged in the course of any such transaction. If the Board of Directors of the Bank decides that counter-obligations cannot be sold advantageously, the income and net proceeds of the investments when finally disposed of shall be distributed to the creditors.

The foregoing power is in addition to the general powers of the Bank to make and realise upon investments for its own account at any time, subject to the provision that such investments are to be made with the assent of the central bank concerned.

(7) To issue its own obligations at long or short term, secured or unsecured, for the purpose of re-lending to any central bank, in each case upon the specific decision of the Board of Directors by a two-thirds vote.

The investment powers of the Bank shall never be used in such a way as to exercise a predominant influence over business interests in any country. The Board of Directors, shall guide the investment undertakings of the Bank accordingly, and shall be entitled if necessary to make special regulations in this respect.

VII.—Trustee Functions: General Provisions

The Bank shall be trustee of the creditor Governments in dealing with the German annuities and shall have such general powers of administration consistent with the Plan as are necessary to the prompt and complete exercise of its duties in that respect. The Organisation Committee shall draw up appropriate forms of trust agreement between the creditor Governments and the Bank.

The trust functions of the Bank shall include the following:

(1) Receiving and disbursing to the paying agents the service on the German External Loan, 1924. If arrangements can legally be made, the Bank shall also act in the capacity of one of the Trustees for that Loan.

(2) Receiving from Germany the various certificates and obligations provided for in the Plan. The Bank shall hold these certificates and obligations in safe keeping and shall issue to the creditors its trust receipts for such certificates and obligations. Upon the completion of the payments called for under these certificates and obligations for any one year, the respective creditor Governments shall give their quittance to the Bank, which in turn shall give its quittance to the German Government, cancelling and returning any coupons representing the payments made.

(3) Receiving and distributing the service of the German annuities. The specifications of this function are given in Section VIII. of this outline below.

(4) Performing as regards Deliveries in Kind such functions as may be entrusted to it by the Governments in connection with the acceptance of the new Plan.

(5) Dealing with the measures of safeguard provided in the Plan. Upon receiving notification from the German Government consistently with the provisions of the Plan the Bank shall convene the Special Advisory Committee whose composition, procedure and action are provided for in Section 8 (e) of the Plan.

(6) Acting as trustee under trust agreements. The Bank shall have the power to act as trustee under trust agreements

L

entered into by it with the approval or on the initiative of its Board of Directors, which has as its purpose the issue by the Bank of trust certificates or other obligations against investments in securities pledged as collateral therefor. This power may be exercised in addition to the powers with respect to investments provided for in Section VI. above.

(7) Acting as trustee under special agreements. The Bank shall be authorised to act as trustee under any special agreements among the creditor countries covering the repartition of the annuities or the guarantee of any parts of them. In particular, the Bank shall have power to act as trustee under the agreement specified in Annex VIII. of the Plan. The Bank shall be authorised to pay interest on any guarantee fund deposited with the Bank in connection with any such trust, and to arrange the terms on which the deposit is to be received and the fund managed, all in accordance with the Plan.

(8) Acting as trustee at the request of a creditor Government, the German Government or the central bank of any one of those countries. The Bank shall have the right, upon the approval of the Board of Directors, to undertake any trust functions which any creditor Government or the German Government or any of their respective central banks proposes that it shall undertake, provided such functions are generally consistent with the purposes of the Plan.

VIII.—TRUSTEE FUNCTIONS: THE BANK AS DEPOSITORY FOR THE SERVICE OF THE GERMAN ANNUITIES

The Bank, in its capacity as trustee for the creditor Governments, shall receive and distribute the funds representing the service of the German annuities. In fulfilling these functions the Bank shall work in co-operation with the central banks of the countries concerned; the relations thus established shall be the ordinary relationships obtaining between a bank and its correspondent banks.

The procedure for conducting these operations, subject to the right of the Board of Directors of the Bank to make modifications provided the general purposes of the Plan are observed, shall be as follows:

(1) The Bank shall maintain on its books a general deposit account to be known as the Annuity Trust Account.

(2) The German Government shall be responsible for the payment to the Bank, in instalments as provided in the Plan, of all sums applicable to the service of the annuity. These payments shall be credited to the Annuity Trust Account.

The Organisation Committee shall make the necessary provision whereby the Reichsmark payments to the account of the Bank at the Reichsbank in respect of the Railway contribution shall be immediately released to the German Government against equivalent payment in foreign currencies to the Annuity Trust Account.

(3) Subject to the operation of the clauses of the Plan relating to transfer postponement, and except as the Bank may request that payments be made in Reichsmarks to the credit of its account at the Reichsbank described in Paragraph 4 below, the German Government shall make all payments on account of the annuity in foreign currencies. Payments in foreign currencies not on a gold or a gold exchange standard shall be made only with the consent of the Bank. As a matter of business practice the Bank, acting in advance of the payment dates, may notify to the German Government or its agent the Bank's preferences with respect to the currencies in which payment may be made. In case the Bank's preferences are not complied with, payment shall be made to the Bank in the currencies of the seven countries whose nationals are members of the present Experts' Committee, divided as nearly as may be in proportion to their respective shares in that portion of the annuity accruing to them.

(4) All Reichsmark payments for credit to the Annuity Trust Account shall be paid into an account of the Bank at the Reichsbank. The Bank shall be entitled to draw upon it in making all Reichsmark payments necessary for the operation of the Plan, including payments for administrative expenses incurred in Germany, payments for deliveries in kind

and any other disbursements on annuity account. The Bank shall also be entitled to withdraw Reichsmarks from this account or to deposit Reichsmarks in it in the course of conducting operations referred to in Paragraph 14 below, and it may open other accounts at the Reichsbank for use in connection therewith. Such additional accounts shall be operated according to ordinary business principles. The Bank shall have available at all times sufficient funds in Reichsmarks to cover current requirements on account of payments for deliveries in kind.

(5) The Bank shall give its receipt to the German Government for all sums which it pays or causes to be paid into the Annuity Trust Account in the course of carrying out its obligations under the Plan. The receipt of the Bank shall make note of the currencies received, but credit shall be given in the Reichsmark equivalent of those currencies. The German Government undertakes, for the purpose of the present provisions, as well as for the general purposes of the Plan, that the Reichsmark shall have and shall retain its convertibility into gold or devisen as contemplated in Section 31 of the present Reichsbank Law, and that for these purposes the Reichsmark shall have and shall retain a mint parity of 1/2790 kilogram of fine gold as defined in the German Coinage Law of August 30, 1924.[1] Sums paid in foreign currencies into the Annuity Trust Account shall be calculated in terms of Reichsmarks at the average of the middle rates (Mittelkurs) prevailing on the Berlin Bourse during the half-monthly period preceding the date of payment.

(6) The Bank's receipt giving credit in Reichsmarks for payments made into the Annuity Trust Account by the German Government or on its behalf shall under normal operation of the Plan constitute a complete and sufficient discharge of the obligations of the German Government with respect to such payments. If, however, transfer postponement should be in whole or partial effect, the Bank's receipt giving credit in Reichsmarks shall constitute a complete and

[1] See the letter from the President of the Reichsbank given in Annex II.

sufficient discharge of the obligations of the German Government with respect to all payments into the Annuity Trust Account made in foreign exchange, and with respect to such portion of the payments made in Reichsmarks as in the opinion of the Bank provide current funds for deliveries in kind or services. As to the remainder, the receipt of the Bank shall be in the nature of a temporary acknowledgment only.

(7) Withdrawals from the Annuity Trust Account shall be made in accordance with provisions to be made by the Organisation Committee. The Bank shall pay no interest on funds deposited in the Annuity Trust Account.

(8) All disbursements for reparation purposes shall be charged against the Annuity Trust Account. A first charge against that account shall be the service currently due on the German External Loan, 1924. The Board of Directors shall be entitled also to charge against the account such sums as they deem to be fair compensation for the services performed by the Bank and such out-of-pocket expenses as it incurs in administering the Plan. If, in the opinion of the Directors, such service charges or costs cannot be equitably charged to the account as a whole, they shall be entitled to allocate them in such proportion as they see fit to the individual shares of any of the creditor countries.

(9) After charging against the Annuity Trust Account the items referred to in the preceding paragraph and such other items as may be properly chargeable to the annuity as a whole, the Bank shall proceed in the following manner with the distribution of the remainder of the available funds to the accounts of the several creditors in accordance with the provisions of the Plan.

(10) During such period of time as payments for deliveries in kind and payments under Reparation Recovery Act and similar procedures continue to be made, the Bank shall make available to the several creditor countries Reichsmark credits, which shall be utilised subject to the applicable provisions of the Plan.

(11) The Bank, out of each instalment paid into the

Annuity Trust Account, shall set aside and accumulate funds for the payment of service on any bonds issued and outstanding which represent commercialised and mobilised shares in the annuity. Funds required for this purpose shall be charged against the accounts of the creditor countries in proportion to their respective interests in the bonds for which service is being accumulated. At a suitable time in advance of the dates fixed for the payment of interest to the bondholders the Bank shall pay to the paying agents the amounts due in interest, and shall make disposition according to the terms of the bond of funds required for purposes of amortisation.

(12) Out of the sums remaining in currencies other than Reichsmarks, and after providing for any other charges called for under the Plan, the Directors of the Bank shall distribute such aggregate amounts as they may determine to the creditor countries, divided according to the proportions agreed upon among the respective Governments. In withholding any sums from distribution and in fixing the dates at which distribution is effected, the Directors of the Bank shall be guided on the one hand by the need for prompt action in the interests of the creditor countries and on the other by the interests of the Plan as a whole, including due consideration to the Bank by way of compensation for its services in managing the annuity.

(13) The Bank shall make distribution of cash by crediting the accounts which the central banks of the several creditor countries maintain with it, notifying them simultaneously that such credits are for the accounts of their respective Governments. The Bank shall notify the proper financial authorities of the creditor countries when such credits have been made, and shall obtain receipts from them accordingly.

(14) The Bank shall have the right to buy for its own account or for other trust accounts any Reichsmarks held in the Annuity Trust Account, giving foreign currencies in return. The foreign currencies thus acquired by the Annuity Trust Account shall be available for distribution to the creditor countries under the conditions specified in the pre-

ceding paragraphs. The Reichsmarks which the Bank acquires shall be used only as the Plan provides.

(15) The Bank, at the close of each business year, or more frequently if requested, shall give to the financial authorities of each creditor country a full accounting showing the disposition of its share in the annuity. As soon as any country has received its full share in the annuity for any one year, its proper financial authority shall give to the Bank his acknowledgment and shall enter the same upon the trust receipt provided for in Paragraph 2 of Section VII. of this outline. Such acknowledgment shall constitute a full and sufficient discharge to the Bank with respect to the annuity covered by it.

IX.—AGENCY FUNCTIONS

The Bank shall be qualified, on terms to be mutually agreed upon, to act as agent and correspondent of any central bank, and to appoint any central bank to act as its agent and correspondent. The services to be performed by either or both parties under such agreements shall be subject, so far as the Bank's interest is concerned, to the approval of its Board of Directors, and may include the purchase and sale of gold, of bills of exchange and other securities, the earmarking of gold, the exchange of information and advice, and the transaction of any business consistent with the functions of the Bank under the Plan on the one hand and within the lawful functions of the central bank on the other.

The Bank shall act as agent of any creditor Government in mobilising any parts of the annuities, and in managing the service of bonds issued in connection with any such mobilisation. The procedure for conducting the Bank's share in such operations, subject to the right of the Organisation Committee of the Board of Directors of the Bank to make modifications provided the general purposes of the Plan are observed, shall be as follows:

(1) Upon the request of the creditor Governments, or any of them, the Bank shall initiate operations for marketing

bonds, if after examination it considers market conditions warrant such operations. Such operations may take place in the international markets, or may be restricted to the domestic market or markets of the countries concerned in the proposed mobilisation, as the Board of Directors may decide. In determining the markets where offerings are to be made, the Bank shall make inquiries from the central banks concerned, and if any central bank offers explicit objection to an offering being made in its own market the Directors shall decide accordingly.

(2) The Bank shall proceed to carry out requests from any creditor Government for the creation of bonds to be issued on its domestic market in connection with conversion operations up to an amount represented in its share in the annuities. Each State shall be free to offer such bonds on its own market on whatever conditions it can obtain.

(3) If in the opinion of the Bank the time is opportune for an issue of bonds, even if no request for mobilisation has been received, the Bank may inform the creditor Governments accordingly.

(4) If the creditor Governments so request, the Bank shall arrange with issuing bankers the conditions upon which bonds are to be issued on the open markets either of one or of several countries, as the case may be. The Bank shall fix the minimum price at which such issues shall be made and it shall supervise the execution of the loan contracts.

(5) If bonds are issued against the annuity shares of more than one country, the proceeds shall be deposited with the Bank, which shall then distribute the proceeds to the creditors according to their participation. The handling of the service of issued bonds shall be carried out as provided in the preceding Section of this outline and in Annex III.

(6) Apart from the operations described above, the Bank may conduct any other operations (such, for instance, as contango operations on bonds issued against the annuities, advances on coupons, &c.) as are involved in the supervision of transactions relating to these bonds and their service.

X.—Reserve Requirements

The Bank, since its deposits in part will be derived from central banks, shall be administered with particular regard to maintaining its liquidity. For this purpose, the Bank shall observe the following reserve requirements:

(1) Deposits on clearing account. All funds held by the Bank on clearing account, whether gold in vault or gold under earmark for the Bank's account in central banks, shall be reserved for exclusive use in effecting settlements among the depositaries in the account.

(2) Deposits payable on demand. Against such deposits the Bank shall hold a minimum of 40 per cent in gold or in devisen at their gold value. Devisen eligible as reserve against demand deposits shall consist of bank-notes; prime bills of exchange having not more than 90 days to run, of a character which central banks ordinarily buy for their own account; and cheques payable on demand, drawn or endorsed by central banks, or in respect of which three obligees, including a bank of known solvency, are responsible. All devisen included in the foregoing classifications shall be denominated in currencies which satisfy, in the opinion of the Board of Directors, all the practical requirements of the gold or gold exchange standard. Gold in transit, or devisen satisfying the foregoing requirements which are in process of collection, may be counted as reserve.

(3) Deposits on investment account. (Time deposits.) Deposits payable in fifteen days or less shall be classified as demand deposits and be subject to the reserve requirements specified in the preceding paragraph. Against investment account deposits of longer maturity the Bank shall hold a minimum of 25 per cent in gold or in devisen at their gold value. Devisen eligible as reserve against investment account deposits shall meet the same requirements as those eligible as reserve against demand deposits.

If the Board of Directors is of opinion that these reserve requirements should be altered, they shall have the right by a two-thirds vote to increase, diminish or otherwise modify them consistently with sound banking principles.

XI.—Distribution of Profits

The yearly net profits of the Bank shall be applied as follows:

(1) Five per cent of the yearly net profits shall be paid to the Legal Reserve Fund of the Bank until that fund reaches an amount equal to 10 per cent of the paid-in capital stock of the Bank as it may stand from time to time. The Legal Reserve Fund on the liquidation of the Bank shall be merged with the General Reserve Fund.

(2) After making the foregoing provision for the Legal Reserve Fund, the yearly net profits shall be applied to the payment of an annual dividend up to 6 per cent on the paid-in share capital. This dividend shall be cumulative.

(3) Twenty per cent of the remainder shall be paid to the shareholders until a total maximum dividend of 12 per cent is reached. The Board of Directors of the Bank shall have the right in any year to withhold all or any part of this addition to the regular dividend, and to place it to the credit of a Special Dividend Reserve Fund for use in maintaining the cumulative dividend provided for in the preceding paragraph or for subsequent distribution to the shareholders.

(4) After making provision for the foregoing, one-half of the yearly net profits then remaining shall be paid into the General Reserve Fund of the Bank until it equals the paid-in capital. Thereafter 40 per cent shall be so applied until the General Reserve Fund equals twice the paid-in capital; 30 per cent until it equals three times the paid-in capital; 20 per cent until it equals four times the paid-in capital; 10 per cent until it equals five times the paid-in capital: and from that point onward, 5 per cent.

The General Reserve Fund shall be available for meeting any losses incurred by the Bank. In case it is not adequate for this purpose, recourse may be had to the Legal Reserve Fund provided for under Paragraph 1. In case the General Reserve Fund, by reason of losses or by reason of an increase in the paid-in capital, falls below the amounts provided for above after having once attained them, the appropriate proportions of the yearly net profits shall again be applied until the position is restored. Upon the liquidation of the Bank, the balance in the General Reserve Fund shall be divided among the shareholders.

(5) The remainder of the yearly net profits after meeting the foregoing requirements shall be paid into Special Funds as follows.

(a) Seventy-five per cent to the Governments or central banks of the creditor countries or of Germany which maintain time deposits at the Bank, withdrawable in not less than five years from the time of deposit, and after four years on not less than one year's notice. The fund shall be disbursed annually in amounts proportionate to the size of the deposits maintained by the respective Governments or central banks aforesaid. The Directors of the Bank shall have power to determine the volume of each of these deposits which would justify the distribution provided for.

(b) Twenty-five per cent to be used to aid Germany in paying the last 22 annuities, provided the German Government elects to make a long-term deposit with the Bank, withdrawable only on the terms specified under Subparagraph (a) above, and amounting to the minimum sum of 400,000,000 Reichsmarks. If the German Government elects to make such long-term deposits amounting to a sum below 400,000,000 Reichsmarks, the participation of the German Government shall be reduced in proportion, and the balance shall be added to the 75 per cent in Subparagraph (a). The fund shall carry compound interest at the maximum current rate paid by the Bank on time deposits. If the fund should exceed the amount required to pay the 22 last annuities, the balance shall be distributed among the creditor Governments in proportion to their out-payments during that period. In case the German Government elects not to make any such long-term deposits, the fund shall be distributed as provided in Subparagraph (a) above.

XII.—General Provisions

Any balances remaining in the hands of the Agent-General for Reparation Payments on the winding-up of his accounts shall be transferred to the Bank for credit to the Annuity Trust Account, subject, of course, to the respective interests of the creditor countries therein and to any claims and commitments which may be outstanding at the time.

The relations of the Reparation Commission with Germany will be terminated. The Bank shall take over as promptly as possible such functions of the Reparation Commission with respect to Germany as are required under the provisions of the Plan, and also such functions of the Agent-General for Reparation Payments, the Trustees and Commissioners holding office under the Experts' Plan of 1924, or any of them, as may be required under the provisions of the Plan, all according to the general scheme given in Part 6 of the Plan and Annex V.

If in any country there is more than one bank of issue, the term "central bank" as used in this outline shall be interpreted to mean the bank of issue situated and operating in the principal financial market of that country.

If in the process of organising the Bank, or in the performance of its functions after establishment, it is found that the central bank of any country or its Governor is unable to act officially or unofficially in any or all of the capacities provided for in this outline, or refrains from so acting, alternative arrangements not inconsistent with the laws of that country shall be made. In particular, the Governors of the central banks of the countries whose nationals are members of the present Committee, or as many of them as are qualified to act, may invite to become members of the Board of Directors of the Bank two nationals of any country the central bank of which is eligible under this outline to take part in forming the Board of the Bank but does not do so. The two nationals of that country upon acceptance of the invitation shall be qualified to act in the full capacity of Directors of the Bank as provided in this outline. Further, the Directors of the Bank shall be authorised to appoint, in lieu of any central bank not exercising any or all of the functions, authorities or privileges which this outline provides that central banks may or shall exercise, any bank or banking house of widely recognised standing and of the same nationality. Such bank or banking house, upon appointment and acceptance, shall be entitled to act in the place of the central bank in any or all capacities appropriate to central banks under this outline, provided only that such action is not inconsistent with the laws of the country in question.

The balance-sheet and accounts of the Bank shall be audited each year by independent auditors of recognised standing, who shall be appointed by and report to the Board of Directors.

In case the measures proposed in the Plan with respect to the avoidance of double and triple taxation of the Bank are not fully in effect when the Bank begins operations, the Board of Directors shall deal with the matter within its discretion.

If any administrative act of the Bank or any decision of the Board of Directors is disputed on the ground that it is inconsistent with the provisions or intent of the Plan, recourse may be had to arbitration under the general provisions for arbitration.

ANNEX III

MOBILISATION

I.—Form of Indebtedness

Germany's debt shall be fixed in the form of annuities. A certificate of indebtedness representative of these annuities shall be delivered by Germany to the Bank as trustee of the creditor Powers.

To this certificate of indebtedness shall be attached coupons representative of each annuity payable by Germany. Each annuity coupon shall be divided into two parts: the first, representative of that portion of the annuity not subject to postponement and corresponding to the portion of Germany's indebtedness which is mobilisable; the second, representative of that portion of the annuity which is subject to postponement and corresponding to the portion of Germany's indebtedness which is not mobilisable. Each part of the annuity coupon enjoys equal rights throughout, except with respect to the agreed privilege of postponement.

II.—Bond Issues

Upon the request of all or of any one of the creditor Governments, the Bank, as trustee, if it considers such a course opportune, has the right to require the creation of, and the German Government is obliged to create, issuable bonds representing the capitalisation of any part of the portion of the annuity coupons not subject to postponement.

The Bank, however, is obliged, under the provisions set forth in Paragraph VII. (*d*), to accede to requests for the creation of bonds made to it by Governments which are desirous of undertaking internal issues of German bonds in connection with conversion operations.

The certificates of indebtedness, the coupons attached thereto, and such bonds as shall be issued in capitalisation of any parts of the annuities not subject to postponement, shall be made out in the name of the German Reich and shall represent the obligation of the Reich guaranteed by its general revenues.

III.—Collateral Guarantees

A. The Railway Company shall deposit with the Bank for International Settlements a certificate acknowledging its liability in respect of the obligations laid down in Part 8 (*a*) of this Plan.

B. The Reich, furthermore, shall undertake to assign certain revenues (customs and certain taxes on consumption) for the service of the certificates and, as far as they may be exchanged into negotiable bonds, for the service of such bonds. This assignment will constitute a negative pledge and will be ruled by the following conditions:

(*a*) The assigned revenues as estimated for the Budget, 1929, must have a total yield of not less than 150 per cent of the highest budgetary contribution payable by Germany under this plan.

(*b*) The Reich will not pledge the assigned revenues for any other loan or credit, except with the consent of the Bank. If the assigned revenues should be pledged, with the consent of the Bank, for any other loan or credit, the charge for reparation payment will rank ahead of the charge for such other loan or credit.

(*c*) If at any time the total yield of the assigned revenues should fall below 150 per cent of the highest budgetary contribution payable by Germany under this Plan, the Bank may require that additional revenues, sufficient to assure the immediate restoration of the yield to the above percentage, be assigned.

IV.—General Form of the Bonds

The value of the issuable bonds may, according to circumstances, be expressed in dollars, equivalent to so many pounds, Reichsmarks, francs, etc., or inversely in pounds, in Reichsmarks, in francs, etc., always provided that the principal of any bond issued in a particular market shall be payable only in the currency of that market at the equivalent of its gold value.

The coupons shall be expressed in dollars, pounds, francs, etc., and shall be payable at the rate of the day on all the markets on which the bonds are quoted.

In the event of an issue, the amount and form of bonds to be created, as well as the specification of the currency in which they shall be issued, shall be fixed by the Bank in accordance with the requests which it receives from the creditor Governments, taking into account the desiderata of the issuing bankers.

After a period of 10 years, the Bank, in agreement with the issuing bankers and the creditor Governments, may consider the issue of bonds the service of which may be paid in different currencies at par at the bearer's option.

V.—Status of Mobilisable Portions of Annuity Coupons

The service of interest and amortisation of the mobilisable or mobilised portions of the annuity coupons shall be paid to the Bank in foreign currencies by the German Reich without any reservation, *i.e.*, on its own responsibility ; the financial service of these mobilisable or mobilised portions of the annuities shall constitute a final, absolute and unconditional international obligation in the ordinary financial sense of the word.

VI.—Status of Non-Mobilisable Portions of the Annuity Coupons

The payment of the non-mobilisable portion of the annuity coupons shall be made to the Bank by the German Government on the same conditions as that of the mobilised or mobilisable portion of the annuity coupons.

Nevertheless:

1. Bonds representing the non-mobilisable portion of the annuity coupons cannot be created except with the consent of the German Government.

2. It is in respect of the non-mobilisable portion of the annuity coupons that the German Government may avail itself of the right of postponing transfer or payment granted elsewhere in this Plan.

VII.—Functions of the Bank

(a) *Supervision of Agreements*

It shall supervise, both on behalf of the creditor Governments and the bondholders and on behalf of the debtor Government, the strict execution of the agreements concluded between them on the established bases.

(b) *Distribution without Priority*

The Bank shall distribute moneys in payment of the mobilised or mobilisable portions of the annuity coupons among the whole of the bondholders and the creditor Governments in proportion to the rights of each to share in the portion of the annuity coupons not subject to postponement, without allowing a priority of any kind to any *tranche* or to any claim. It will distribute the moneys relating to the non-mobilisable portions of the annuity coupons amongst the creditor Governments, the transfer of these moneys taking place only after the transfer of the moneys relating to the mobilised or mobilisable portion of the annuity coupons.

(c) *Issue of Bonds on the Markets*

The Bank shall inform the creditor Governments whenever the issue of bonds representing the capitalisation of some part of the mobilisable portion of the annuity coupons is practicable, in its opinion.

It will be the function of the Bank to fix the minimum price of issue.

Each of the creditor Governments shall be entitled, but not obliged, to issue its share of the bonds in its own country. It may come to an understanding with the bankers of another country to cede to them all or part of this share, but these bankers shall be obliged to proceed to this issue only on the minimum conditions fixed by the Bank. Any of these Governments may also refuse to allow its quota to be created; in that event the portion of the annuity corresponding to this quota shall continue to be paid to the Governments in question as before.

(d) *Issue of Conversion Bonds*

Creditor Governments desiring to proceed to internal issues of German bonds, in connection with operations for the conversion of National Debt, shall have the option of asking the Bank to create bonds representing all or part of their quota of the mobilisable portion of the annuity coupons. These bonds shall constitute national *tranches* which each Government shall be free to offer on its own market on whatever conditions it can obtain. These bonds shall be quoted only on their market of issue. The service of these bonds shall, however, be effected *pari passu* with that of the other bonds. The coupons of these bonds shall be expressed in pounds, dollars, French francs, etc.,

M

and shall be payable at the rate of the day on all the markets on which the mobilisable bonds are quoted.

———

EXTRACTS FROM ANNEX IV

CONDITIONS OF POSTPONEMENT OF TRANSFER AND OF PAYMENT

4.—UTILISATION OF REICHSMARKS

Any sum in Reichsmarks the transfer of which is postponed shall (save as provided for in Section 3 above) be deposited to the account of the Bank for International Settlements at the Reichsbank for eventual release of balances, not absorbed by deliveries in kind, against payment in foreign currencies by the German Government. At all times, the employment, whether for investment or as indicated below, of Reichsmarks so deposited shall be subject to agreement between the Reichsbank and the Bank for International Settlements. In determining the manner in which these sums shall be employed, regard shall be had to the possibilities that special programmes of deliveries in kind can be arranged with the German Government:

(*a*) During the first ten years, by restricting or extending the programme of deliveries in kind laid down for those years;

(*b*) after the first ten years, by arranging a special programme of deliveries in kind, where the interests of particular industries in Germany and of particular creditor countries which would otherwise suffer may be met without prejudice to the general situation;

provided, however, that any special arrangement which may be made between any creditor country and Germany with a view to reserving to the said creditor the right to receive certain deliveries in kind in case of moratorium shall be carried through subject to a copy of the agreement therefor being communicated to the Bank for International Settlements.

EXTRACTS FROM ANNEX V

ORGANISATION COMMITTEES

1. Just as the Dawes Plan was put into force by the agreement of the Governments concerned laid down in the London Protocol, the New Plan will have to be put into force by agreement of the Governments.

Once the Governments have accepted in principle the New Plan, it seems advisable that, in addition to any preparatory measures necessary for the Conference of the Governments, steps should be taken for the elaboration of detailed schemes about certain technical questions.

Generally speaking, it seems advisable to have these schemes elaborated by special organisation committees, which should be composed substantially in the same way as the organisation committees of the Dawes Plan, *i.e.*, by the same number of representatives of the creditors as of the debtor, with a neutral Chairman to be called in case of disagreement. The Organisation Committee for the New Bank would, however, be differently composed.

We recommend such organisation committees for the following questions:

(1) Organisation Committee for the New Bank, as provided for in Annex I. of the Report.

As there is only one new organisation, which is going to centralise all the various functions concerning the execution of the New Plan, viz., the Bank for International Settlements, it is necessary to provide one special body only for the setting up of this organisation, this body to be the Organisation Committee for the New Bank referred to above, as provided for in Annex I.

The task of transferring the functions of the existing organisations to the Bank for International Settlements should be conferred upon a small special committee, composed of two members of the Organisation Committee for the Bank for International Settlements, as well as of representatives of the German Government, the Agent-General and the Reparation Commission, an equitable representation being assured to the Powers represented upon the present Committee.

ANNEX VIII

GUARANTEE FUND IN RESPECT OF UNCONDITIONAL ANNUITIES

1. The experts of the principal creditor Governments have agreed that there shall be assigned to France out of the unconditional annuity 500 million R.M., in order to allow her to mobilise a substantial part of her share in the total annuity.

The aforesaid experts consider that this assignment should be final, and in no case subject to diminution, but should continue to be included in the total assigned to France subject only to the alteration contemplated in the Special Memorandum signed concurrently with the Report of this Committee.

2. In order to equalise the short payments to other creditors which would arise from a postponement of the postponable portion of the annuity, it was agreed that France should deposit a special guarantee fund with the Bank for International Settlements.

3. On the coming into force of this Plan, France will give to the Bank for International Settlements an undertaking to deposit in a Trust Fund, on the demand of the Bank for International Settlements, foreign currencies to a total value of 500 million R.M. It is understood that this demand will not be made until action has been taken leading to the calling of the Advisory Committee referred to in Section 8 (e) of the Report. The amount of 500 million R.M. will be reduced by the amount of any payments made by France under (4) below. The Bank for International Settlements may retain this deposit as long as it deems necessary, but shall pay interest on it at its maximum current rate for long-term deposits. This deposit, if it is agreed that it shall remain for more than five years, shall be entitled to participate in the profits of the Bank divisible under Part XI. (5) of Annex I.

4. As soon as mobilisation of any part of the French annuity has been effected, France will deduct from the proceeds 10 per cent thereof, or 500 million R.M., whichever is the less, and will deposit it to the credit of the Trust Account of the Bank for International Settlements referred to in the preceding paragraph.

5. Upon postponement of transfer of any payment due from Germany, the Bank for International Settlements shall take the following steps:

(a) Offer to the creditors, other than France, devisen up to the amount necessary (but not exceeding 500 million R.M., divided if necessary proportionately) to ensure to each of them receipts in devisen equal to the amounts they would have received had the non-postponable annuity been distributed in the same proportions as the total annuity.

(b) Debit the Trust Fund set up under (2) above with the amount of devisen actually utilised under paragraph (a).

(c) Receive from each creditor, in exchange for devisen accepted under paragraph (a), an assignment in favour of the Trust Fund of an equivalent amount of the annuity, transfer of which has been postponed.

6. As and when Germany effectively transfers the postponed amounts, the Bank will credit to the Trust Fund its share thereof in accordance with the assignment in (5) (c) above.

APPENDIX III

STATUTES OF THE BANK FOR INTERNATIONAL SETTLEMENTS

The following is the full text of the statutes of the Bank for International Settlements, as adopted at The Hague Conference in January, 1930.

CHAPTER I.—NAME, SEAT AND OBJECTS

Article 1

There is constituted under the name of the Bank for International Settlements (hereinafter referred to as the Bank) a Company limited by shares.

Article 2

The registered office of the Bank shall be situated at Basle, Switzerland.

Article 3

The objects of the Bank are:
to promote the co-operation of central banks and to provide additional facilities for international financial operations; and to act as Trustee or Agent in regard to international financial settlements entrusted to it under agreements with the parties concerned.

Article 4

As long as the New Plan as defined in The Hague Agreement of January, 1930 (hereinafter referred to as the Plan) is in force, the Bank (i) shall carry out the functions assigned

166

to it in the Plan; (ii) shall conduct its affairs with a view to facilitating the execution of the Plan; and (iii) shall observe the provisions of the Plan in the administration and operations of the Bank—all within the limits of the powers granted by the statutes.

During the said period the Bank, as Trustee or Agent for the Governments concerned, shall receive, administer and distribute the annuities paid by Germany under the Plan; shall supervise and assist in the commercialisation and mobilisation of certain portions of the aforesaid annuities; and shall perform such services in connection with the payment of German reparations and the international settlements connected therewith as may be agreed upon by the Bank with the Governments concerned.

Chapter II.—Capital

Article 5

The authorised capital of the Bank shall be 500,000,000 gold Swiss francs, equivalent to 145,161,290.32 grammes fine gold.

It shall be divided into 200,000 shares of equal gold nominal value.

The nominal value of each share shall also be expressed on the face of each share in terms both of gold Swiss francs and of the currency of the country in which it is issued, converted at the gold mint parity.

Article 6

The subscription of the total authorised capital having been guaranteed in equal parts by the Banque Nationale de Belgique, the Bank of England, the Banque de France, the Reichsbank, the Banca d'Italia, Messrs. X acting in place of the Bank of Japan, and Messrs. Y, New York, the Bank may begin business as soon as a minimum of 112,000 shares has been subscribed.

Article 7

(1) During the two years following incorporation the Board of Directors of the Bank (hereinafter referred to as the Board)

shall arrange for the subscription of any unissued portion of the authorised capital.

(2) This unissued portion may be offered to the central banks or other banks of countries which have not participated in the original subscription. The selection of countries in which such shares shall be offered for subscription and the amount to be subscribed in each shall be determined by the Board by a two-thirds majority, provided that offers of shares shall only be made in countries interested in Reparations or in countries whose currencies, in the opinion of the Board, satisfy the practical requirements of the gold or gold exchange standard, and that the amount issued in any one of these countries shall not exceed 8000 shares.

(3) The seven banking institutions mentioned in Article 6 shall, in accordance with their several guarantees, subscribe or arrange for the subscription in equal proportions of any part of the authorised capital which at the end of two years remains unsubscribed.

Article 8

(1) Twenty-five per cent only of the value of each share shall be paid up at the time of subscription. The balance may be called up at a later date or dates at the discretion of the Board. Three months' notice shall be given of any such calls.

(2) If a shareholder fails to pay any call on a share on the day appointed for payment thereof, the Board may, after giving reasonable notice to such shareholder, forfeit the share in respect of which the call remains unpaid. A forfeited share may be sold on such terms and in such manner as the Board may think fit; and the Board may execute a transfer in favour of the person or corporation to whom the share is sold. The proceeds of sale may be received by the Bank, which will pay to the defaulting shareholder any part of the net proceeds over and above the amount of the call due and unpaid.

Article 9

(1) The capital of the Bank may be increased or reduced on the proposal of the Board acting by a two-thirds ma-

jority and adopted by a two-thirds majority of the General
Meeting.

(2) In the event of an increase in the authorised capital of the
Bank and of a further issue of shares, the distribution among
countries shall be decided by a two-thirds majority of the
Board. The central banks of Belgium, England, France, Germany, Italy, Japan, and the U.S.A., or some other financial
institution of the last-named country acceptable to the foregoing central banks, shall be entitled to subscribe or arrange
for the subscription in equal proportions of at least 55 per cent
of such additional shares.

(3) No part of the amount not taken by the banks of these
seven countries shall be subscribed in any other country unless
it is interested in Reparations or at the time of issue its currency,
in the opinion of the Board, satisfies the practical requirements
of the gold or gold exchange standard.

Article 10

In extending invitations to subscribe for capital in accordance with Article 7, paragraph 2, or with Article 9, consideration shall be given by the Board to the desirability of associating
with the Bank the largest possible number of central banks.

Article 11

No shares shall be issued below par.

Article 12

The liability of shareholders is limited to the nominal value of
their shares.

Article 13

The shares shall be registered and transferable in the books of
the Bank.

The Bank shall be entitled, without assigning any reason, to
decline to accept any person or corporation as the transferee of
a share. It shall not transfer shares without the prior consent
of the central bank or the institution acting in lieu of a central
bank by or through whom the shares in question were issued.

Article 14

The shares shall carry equal rights to participate in the profits of the Bank and in any distribution of its assets under Articles 53, 54, and 55 of the statutes.

Article 15

The ownership of shares of the Bank carries no right of voting or representation at the General Meeting. The right of representation and of voting, in proportion to the number of shares subscribed in each country, may be exercised by the central bank of that country or by its nominee. Should the central bank of any country not desire to exercise these rights, they may be exercised by a financial institution of widely recognised standing and of the same nationality, appointed by the Board and not objected to by the central bank of the country in question. In cases where there is no central bank, these rights may be exercised, if the Board thinks fit, by an appropriate financial institution of the country in question, appointed by the Board.

Article 16

Any subscribing institution or banking group may issue or cause to be issued to the public the shares for which it has subscribed.

Article 17

Any subscribing institution or banking group may issue to the public certificates against shares of the Bank owned by it. The form, details and terms of issue of such certificates shall be determined by the Bank issuing them, in agreement with the Board.

Article 18

The receipt or ownership of shares of the Bank or of certificates issued in accordance with Article 17 implies acceptance of the statutes of the Bank, and a statement to that effect shall be embodied in the text of such shares and certificates.

Article 19

The registration of the name of a holder of shares in the books of the Bank establishes the title to ownership of the shares so registered.

CHAPTER III.—POWERS OF THE BANK

Article 20

The operations of the Bank shall be in conformity with the monetary policy of the central banks of the countries concerned.

Before any financial operation is carried out by or on behalf of the Bank on a given market or in a given currency, the Board shall afford to the central bank or central banks directly concerned an opportunity to dissent. In the event of disapproval being expressed within such reasonable time as the Board shall specify, the proposed operation shall not take place. A central bank may make its concurrence subject to conditions and may limit its assent to a specific operation, or enter into a general arrangement permitting the Bank to carry on its operations within such limits as to time, character and amount as may be specified. This Article shall not, however, be read as requiring the assent of any central bank to the withdrawal from its market of funds to the introduction of which no objection had been raised by it, in the absence of stipulations to the contrary by the central bank concerned at the time the original operation was carried out.

Any Governor of a central bank, or his alternate or any other Director specially authorised by the central bank of the country in which he is a national to act on its behalf in this matter, shall, if he is present at the meeting of the Board and does not vote against any such proposed operation, be deemed to have given the valid assent of the central bank in question.

If the representative of the central bank in question is absent or if a central bank is not directly represented on the Board, steps shall be taken to afford the central bank or banks concerned an opportunity to express dissent.

Article 21

The operations of the Bank for its own account shall only be carried out in currencies which, in the opinion of the Board, satisfy the practical requirements of the gold or gold exchange standard.

Article 22

The Board shall determine the nature of the operations to be undertaken by the Bank. The Bank may in particular:

(a) buy and sell gold coin or bullion for its own account or for the account of central banks;

(b) hold gold for its own account under earmark in central banks;

(c) accept the custody of gold for account of central banks;

(d) make advances to or borrow from central banks against gold, bills of exchange and other short-term obligations of prime liquidity or other approved securities;

(e) discount, re-discount, purchase or sell, with or without its endorsement, bills of exchange, cheques and other short-term obligations of prime liquidity, including Treasury bills and other such Government short-term securities as are currently marketable;

(f) buy and sell exchange for its own account or for the account of central banks;

(g) buy and sell negotiable securities other than shares for its own account or for the account of central banks;

(h) discount for central banks bills taken from their portfolio and re-discount with central banks bills taken from its own portfolio;

(i) open and maintain current or deposit accounts with central banks;

(j) accept:

  (i) deposits from central banks on current or deposit account;

  (ii) deposits in connection with trustee agreements that may be made between the Bank and Governments in connection with international settlements;

  (iii) such other deposits as, in the opinion of the Board, come within the scope of the Bank's functions.

The Bank may also:

(k) act as agent or correspondent of any central bank;

(*l*) arrange with any central bank for the latter to act as its agent or correspondent. If a central bank is unable or unwilling to act in this capacity, the Bank may make other arrangements, provided that the central bank concerned does not object. If, in such circumstances, it should be deemed advisable that the Bank should establish its own agency, the sanction of a two-thirds majority of the Board will be required;

(*m*) enter into agreements to act as Trustee or Agent in connection with international settlements, provided that such agreements shall not encroach on the obligations of the Bank towards third parties; and carry out the various operations laid down therein.

Article 23

Any of the operations which the Bank is authorised to carry out with central banks under the preceding Article may be carried out with banks, bankers, corporations or individuals of any country, provided that the central bank of that country does not object.

Article 24

The Bank may enter into special agreements with central banks to facilitate the settlement of international transactions between them.

For this purpose it may arrange with central banks to have gold earmarked for their account and transferable on their order, to open accounts through which central banks can transfer their assets from one currency to another, and to take such measures as the Board may think advisable within the limits of the powers granted by these statutes. The principles and rules governing such accounts shall be fixed by the Board.

Article 25

The Bank may not:

(*a*) issue notes payable at sight to bearer;

(*b*) "accept" bills of exchange;

(*c*) make advances to Governments;

(*d*) open current accounts in the name of Governments;

(*e*) acquire a predominant interest in any business concern;

(*f*) except so far as is necessary for the conduct of its own business, remain the owner of real property for any longer period than is required in order to realise to proper advantage such real property as may come into the possession of the Bank in satisfaction of claims due to it.

Article 26

The Bank shall be administered with particular regard to maintaining its liquidity, and for this purpose shall retain assets appropriate to the maturity and character of its liabilities. Its short-term liquid assets may include bank-notes, cheques payable on sight drawn on first class banks, claims in course of collection, deposits at sight or at short notice in first class banks, and prime bills of exchange of not more than ninety days' usance, of a kind usually accepted for re-discount by central banks.

The proportion of the Bank's assets held in any given currency shall be determined by the Board with due regard to the liabilities of the Bank.

Chapter IV.—Management

Article 27

The administration of the Bank shall be vested in the Board.

Article 28

The Board shall be composed as follows:

(1) The Governors for the time being of the central banks of Belgium, France, Germany, Great Britain, Italy, Japan and the United States of America (hereinafter referred to as *ex officio* Directors), or if any of the said Governors are unwilling or unable to hold office, their respective nominees (hereinafter referred to as substitute nominees).

The tenure of office of a substitute nominee shall be within the discretion of the Governor by whom he is appointed, but shall terminate in any case when that Governor vacates office.

Any *ex officio* Director may appoint one person as his alternate, who shall be entitled to attend and exercise the powers of a Director at meetings of the Board if the Governor himself is unable to be present.

(2) Seven persons representative of finance, industry or commerce, appointed one each by the Governors of the central banks mentioned in sub-clause (1) and being of the same nationality as the Governors who appoint them.

During the continuance of the liability of Germany to pay reparation annuities, two persons, of French and German nationality respectively, representative of industry or commerce, appointed by the Governors of the Bank of France and of the Reichsbank respectively, if they so desire.

If for any reason the Governor of any of the seven institutions above mentioned is unable or unwilling to serve as Director, or to appoint a substitute nominee under sub-clause (1), or to make an appointment under sub-clause (2), the Governors of the other institutions referred to, or a majority of them, may invite to become members of the Board two nationals of the country of the Governor in question, not objected to by the central bank of that country.

Directors appointed as aforesaid, other than *ex officio* Directors or their substitute nominees, shall hold office for three years, but shall be eligible for reappointment.

(3) Not more than nine persons to be elected by the following procedure:

The Governor of the central bank of every country, other than those mentioned in sub-clause (1), in which capital has been subscribed at the time of incorporation shall be entitled to submit a list of four candidates of his own nationality for directorship, which may include his own name. Two of the candidates on each list shall be representative of finance, and the other two of industry or commerce. From these lists the Board may elect, by a two-thirds majority, not more than nine persons.

The Directors so elected shall be divided by lot into three

groups, as nearly as may be equal in number, of which one group shall retire at the end of the first, one at the end of the second, and one at the end of the third financial year of the Bank. The retiring Directors shall be eligible for re-election.

At the first meeting of Directors in the second and succeeding financial years the Board may elect, by a two-thirds majority, not more than three Directors from a panel of candidates composed of lists of persons with similar qualifications to those specified in connection with the first election. The Governors of the central banks of every country, other than those mentioned in sub-clause (1), in which capital has at the date of such meeting been subscribed shall be entitled to submit a list of four persons to be included in the panel. Directors so elected shall hold office for three years, but shall be eligible for re-election.

If in any of the countries referred to in the preceding paragraph there is no central bank, the Board, by a two-thirds majority, may nominate an appropriate financial institution to exercise the right of submitting a list of candidates for election.

Article 29

In the event of a vacancy occurring on the Board for any reason other than the termination of a period of office in accordance with the preceding Article, the vacancy shall be filled in accordance with the procedure by which the member to be replaced was selected. In the case of Directors other than *ex officio* Directors, the new Director shall hold office for the unexpired period only of his predecessor's term of office. He shall, however, be eligible for re-election at the expiration of that term.

Article 30

Directors must be ordinarily resident in Europe or in a position to attend regularly at meetings of the Board.

Article 31

No person shall be appointed or hold office as a Director who is a member or an official of a Government, or is a member of a legislative body, unless he is the Governor of a central bank.

Article 32

Meetings of the Board shall be held not less than ten times a year. At least four of these shall be held at the registered office of the Bank.

Article 33

A member of the Board who is not present in person at a meeting of Directors may give a proxy to any other member authorising him to vote at that meeting on his behalf.

Article 34

Unless otherwise provided by the statutes, decisions of the Board shall be taken by a simple majority of those present or represented by proxy. In the case of an equality of votes, the Chairman shall have a second or casting vote.

The Board shall not be competent to act unless a quorum of Directors is present. This quorum shall be laid down in a regulation adopted by a two-thirds majority of the Board.

Article 35

The members of the Board may receive, in addition to out-of-pocket expenses, a fee for attendance at meetings and/or a remuneration, the amounts of which will be fixed by the Board, subject to the approval of the General Meeting.

Article 36

The proceedings of the Board shall be summarised in minutes, which shall be signed by the Chairman.

Copies of or extracts from these minutes for the purpose of production in a Court of Justice must be certified by the General Manager of the Bank.

A record of decisions taken at each meeting shall be sent within eight days of the meeting to every member.

Article 37

The Board shall represent the Bank in its dealings with third parties, and shall have the exclusive right of entering into

N

engagements on behalf of the Bank. It may, however, delegate this right to a member or members of the Board or of the permanent staff of the Bank, provided that it defines the powers of each person to whom it delegates this right.

Article 38

The Bank shall be legally committed *vis-à-vis* third parties by the signature of the President or by two signatures either of members of the Board or of members of the staff who have been duly authorised by the Board to sign on its behalf.

Article 39

The Board shall elect from among its members a Chairman and one or more Vice-Chairmen, one of whom shall preside at meetings of the Board in the absence of the Chairman.

The Chairman of the Board shall be President of the Bank.

He shall hold office for three years, and shall be eligible for re-election.

Subject to the authority of the Board, the President will carry out the policy and control the administration of the Bank.

He shall not hold any other office which, in the judgment of the Board, might interfere with his duties as President.

Article 40

At the meeting of the Board at which the election of a Chairman is to take place, the chair shall be taken by the oldest member of the Board present.

Article 41

A General Manager shall be appointed by the Board on the proposal of the President. He will be responsible to the President for the operations of the Bank, and will be the chief of its operating staff.

The Heads of Departments, and any other officers of similar rank, shall be appointed by the Board on recommendations made by the President after consultation with the General Manager.

The remainder of the staff shall be appointed by the General Manager with the approval of the President.

Article 42

The departmental organisation of the Bank shall be determined by the Board.

Article 43

The Board may, if it thinks fit, appoint from among its members an Executive Committee to assist the President in the administration of the Bank.

The President shall be a member and *ex officio* Chairman of this Committee.

Article 44

The Board may appoint advisory committees, chosen wholly or partly from persons not concerned in the Bank's management.

Article 45

As long as the Plan is in force, the Board shall convene the Special Advisory Committee referred to in the Plan, upon receipt of the notice therein provided for.

CHAPTER V.—GENERAL MEETINGS

Article 46

General Meetings of the Bank may be attended by nominees of the central banks or other financial institutions referred to in Article 15.

Voting rights shall be in proportion to the number of shares subscribed in the country of each institution represented at the meeting.

The chair shall be taken at General Meetings by the Chairman of the Board, or in his absence by a Vice-Chairman.

At least three weeks' notice of General Meetings shall be given to those entitled to be represented.

Subject to the provisions of these statutes, the General Meeting shall decide upon its own procedure.

Article 47

Within three months after the end of each financial year of the Bank, an Annual General Meeting shall be held, upon such date as the Board may decide.

The meeting shall take place at the registered office of the Bank.

Voting by proxy will be permitted in such manner as the Board may have provided in advance by regulation.

Article 48

The Annual General Meeting shall be invited:

(a) to approve the Annual Report, the Balance-Sheet upon the report of the auditors, and the Profit and Loss Account, and any proposed changes in the remuneration, fees or allowances of the members of the Board;

(b) to make appropriations to reserve and to special funds, and to consider the declaration of a dividend and its amount;

(c) to elect the auditors for the ensuing year and to fix their remuneration; and

(d) to discharge the Board from all personal responsibility in respect of the past financial year.

Article 49

Extraordinary General Meetings shall be summoned to decide upon any proposals of the Board:

(a) to amend the statutes;

(b) to increase or decrease the capital of the Bank;

(c) to liquidate the Bank.

CHAPTER VI.—ACCOUNTS AND PROFITS

Article 50

The financial year of the Bank will begin on 1st April and end on 31st March. The first financial period will end on 31st March 1931.

Article 51

The Bank shall publish an Annual Report, and at least once a month a Statement of Account in such form as the Board may prescribe.

The Board shall cause to be prepared a Profit and Loss Account and Balance-Sheet of the Bank for each financial year in time for submission to the Annual General Meeting.

Article 52

The Accounts and Balance-Sheet shall be audited by independent auditors. The auditors shall have full power to examine all books and accounts of the Bank and to require full information as to all its transactions. The auditors shall report to the Board and to the General Meeting, and shall state in their report:

(a) whether or not they have obtained all the information and explanations they have required; and

(b) whether, in their opinion, the Balance-Sheet dealt with in the report is properly drawn up so as to exhibit a true and correct view of the state of the Bank's affairs, according to the best of their information and the explanations given to them, and as shown by the books of the Bank.

Article 53

The yearly net profits of the Bank shall be applied as follows:

(a) five per cent of such net profits, or such proportion of five per cent as may be required for the purpose, shall be paid to a reserve fund called the Legal Reserve Fund, until that fund reaches an amount equal in value to ten per cent of the amount of the paid-up capital of the Bank for the time being;

(b) thereafter such net profits shall be applied in or towards the payment of a dividend of six per cent per annum on the amount of the paid-up capital of the Bank: this dividend shall be cumulative;

(c) as to the residue (if any) of such net profits, twenty per cent shall be paid to the shareholders until a maximum further dividend of six per cent (which shall be non-cumulative) is reached, provided that the Board may in any year withhold all or any part of this additional payment and place it to the credit of a Special Dividend Reserve Fund for use in maintaining the cumulative six per cent dividend provided for in the preceding paragraph or for subsequent distribution to the shareholders;

(d) after making provision for the foregoing, one-half of the yearly net profits then remaining shall be paid into the General Reserve Fund of the Bank until it equals the paid-up capital. Thereafter forty per cent shall be so applied until the General Reserve Fund equals twice the paid-up capital; thirty per cent until it equals three times the paid-up capital; twenty per cent until it equals four times the paid-up capital; ten per cent until it equals five times the paid-up capital; and from that point onward, five per cent.

In case the General Reserve Fund, by reason of losses or by reason of an increase in the paid-up capital, falls below the amounts provided for above after having once attained them, the appropriate proportion of the yearly net profits shall again be applied until the position is restored;

(e) as long as the Plan is in force any remainder of the net profits after meeting the foregoing requirements shall be disposed of as follows:

(i) as to seventy-five per cent, to such of the Governments or central banks of Germany and the countries entitled to share in the annuities payable under the Plan as have maintained time deposits at the Bank subject to withdrawal in not less than five years from the time of deposit, or after four years on not less than one year's notice. This sum shall be distributed annually in proportion to the size of the deposits maintained by the respective Governments or central banks in question. The Board shall have the power to determine the minimum deposit which would justify the distribution provided for;

(ii) as to twenty-five per cent as follows:

If the German Government elects to make a long-term deposit with the Bank withdrawable only on the terms specified under sub-clause (i) above, and amounting to the minimum sum of 400,000,000 Reichsmarks, the said twenty-five per cent shall go into a Special Fund, to be used to aid Germany in paying the last twenty-two annuities provided for in the Plan.

If the German Government elects to make such long-term deposit amounting to a sum below 400,000,000 Reichsmarks, the participation of the German Government shall be reduced in proportion, and the balance shall be added to the seventy-five per cent referred to in sub-clause (i) above.

If the German Government elects not to make any such long-term deposit, the said twenty-five per cent shall be distributed as provided in sub-clause (i) above. The Special Fund referred to above shall carry compound interest reckoned on an annual basis at the maximum current rate paid by the Bank on time deposits.

If the Special Fund should exceed the amount required to pay the last twenty-two annuities, the balance shall be distributed among the creditor Governments as provided for in the Plan.

(f) At the expiration of the period referred to in the first paragraph of sub-clause (e) the disposal of the remainder of the net profits referred to in sub-clause (e) shall be determined by the General Meeting on the proposal of the Board.

Article 54

The General Reserve Fund shall be available for meeting any losses incurred by the Bank. In case it is not adequate for this purpose, recourse may be had to the Legal Reserve Fund provided for in Article 53 (a).

These reserve funds in the event of liquidation, and after

the discharge of the liabilities of the Bank and the costs of liquidation, shall be divided among the shareholders.

CHAPTER VII.—GENERAL PROVISIONS

Article 55

The Bank may not be liquidated except by a three-fourths majority of the General Meeting. It shall not in any case be liquidated before it has discharged all the obligations which it has assumed under the Plan.

Article 56

(1) If any dispute shall arise between the Bank, on the one side, and any central bank, financial institution, or other bank referred to in the present statutes, on the other side, or between the Bank and its shareholders, with regard to the interpretation or application of the statutes of the Bank, the same shall be referred for final decision to the Tribunal provided for by The Hague Agreement of January, 1930.

(2) In the absence of agreement as to the terms of submission, either party to a dispute under this Article may refer the same to the Tribunal, which shall have power to decide all questions (including the question of its own jurisdiction) even in default of appearance by the other party.

(3) The Tribunal shall lay down its own procedure.

(4) Before giving a final decision and without prejudice to the questions at issue, the President of the Tribunal—or, if he is unable to act in any case, a member of the Tribunal to be designated by him forthwith—may, on the request of the first party applying therefor, order any appropriate provisional measures in order to safeguard the respective rights of the parties.

(5) The provisions of this Article shall not prejudice the right of the parties to a dispute to refer the same by common consent to the President or a member of the Tribunal as sole arbitrator.

Article 57

In all cases not covered by the preceding Article or by some other provision for arbitration the Bank may proceed or be proceeded against in any court of competent jurisdiction.

Article 58

For the purposes of these statutes:

(1) Central bank means the bank in any country to which has been entrusted the duty of regulating the volume of currency and credit in that country; or, where a banking system has been so entrusted, the bank forming part of such system which is situated and operating in the principal financial market of that country.

(2) The Governor of a central bank means the person who, subject to the control of his Board or other competent authority, has the direction of the policy and administration of the Bank.

(3) A two-thirds majority of the Board means not less than two-thirds of the votes (whether given in person or by proxy) of the whole directorate.

Article 59

Amendments of any Articles of these statutes other than those enumerated in Article 60 may be proposed by a two-thirds majority of the Board of Directors to the General Meeting, and, if adopted by a majority of the General Meeting, shall come into force, provided that such amendments are not inconsistent with the provisions of the Articles enumerated in Article 60.

Article 60

Articles 2, 3, 4, 9, 15, 20, 25, 28, 46, 53, 56, 59, and 60 cannot be amended except subject to the following conditions: The amendment must be adopted by a two-thirds majority of the Board, approved by a majority of the General Meeting, and sanctioned by a law supplementing the Charter of the Bank.

APPENDIX IV

CHARTER OF THE BANK FOR INTERNATIONAL SETTLEMENTS

The following is the full text of the Convention regarding the Bank for International Settlements signed at The Hague on January 20, 1930.

THE duly authorised representatives of the Governments of Germany, of Belgium, of France, of the United Kingdom of Great Britain and Northern Ireland, of Italy and of Japan of the one part.

And the duly authorised representatives of the Government of the Swiss Confederation of the other part.

Assembled at The Hague Conference in the month of January, 1930, have agreed on the following:

Article 1

Switzerland undertakes to grant to the Bank for International Settlements, without delay, the following constituent charter having force of law: not to abrogate this charter, not to amend or add to it, and not to sanction amendments to the Statutes of the Bank referred to in paragraph 4 of the charter otherwise than in agreement with the other signatory Governments.

Article 2

Any dispute between the Swiss Government and any one of the other signatory Governments relating to the interpretation or application of the present Convention shall be submitted to the Arbitral Tribunal provided for by The Hague Agreement of

January, 1930. The Swiss Government may appoint a member who shall sit on the occasion of such disputes, the President having a casting vote. In having recourse to this Tribunal the Parties may always agree between themselves to submit their dispute to the President or to one of the members of the Tribunal chosen to act as sole arbiter.

Article 3

The present Convention is entered into for a period of 15 years. It is entered into on the part of Switzerland under reserve of ratification and shall be put into force as soon as it shall have been ratified by the Government of the Swiss Confederation.

The instrument of ratification shall be deposited with the Ministry of Foreign Affairs at Paris. Upon the entry into force of the Convention, the Swiss Government will initiate the necessary constitutional procedure in order that the assent of the Swiss people may be obtained for the maintenance in force during the whole of the Bank's existence of the provisions of the present Convention. As soon as these measures have become fully effective the Swiss Government will notify the other signatory Governments and these provisions shall become valid during the Bank's existence.

CONSTITUENT CHARTER OF THE BANK FOR INTERNATIONAL SETTLEMENTS

Whereas the Powers signatory to The Hague Agreement of January, 1930, have adopted a Plan which contemplates the founding by the Central Banks of Belgium, France, Germany, Great Britain, Italy and Japan and by a financial institution of the United States of America of an International Bank to be called the Bank for International Settlements;

And whereas the said central banks and a banking group including Messrs. J. P. Morgan & Company of New York, the First National Bank of New York, New York, and the First National Bank of Chicago, Chicago have undertaken to found the said Bank and have guaranteed or arranged for the guarantee of the subscription of its authorised capital amounting to five hundred million Swiss Francs equal to 145,161,290.32 gram, fine gold, divided into 200,000 shares;

And whereas the Swiss Federal Government has entered into a treaty with the Governments of Germany, Belgium, France, Great Britain, Italy and Japan whereby the said Federal Government has agreed to grant the present Constituent Charter of the Bank for International Settlements and not to repeal, amend or supplement the said Charter and not to sanction amendments to the Statutes of the Bank referred to in Paragraph 4 of the present Charter except in agreement with the said Powers:

1. The Bank for International Settlements (hereinafter called the Bank) is hereby incorporated.

2. Its constitution, operations and activities are defined and governed by the annexed Statutes which are hereby sanctioned.

3. Amendment of Articles of the said Statutes other than those enumerated in Paragraph 4 hereof may be made and shall be put into force as provided in Article 59 of the said Statutes and not otherwise.

4. Articles 2, 3, 4, 9, 15, 20, 25, 28, 46, 53, 56, 59 and 60 of the said Statutes shall not be amended except subject to the following conditions: the amendment must be adopted by a two-thirds majority of the Board, approved by a majority of the General Meeting and sanctioned by a law supplementing the present Charter.

5. The said Statutes and any amendments which may be made thereto in accordance with Paragraphs 3 or 4 hereof respectively shall be valid and operative notwithstanding any inconsistency therewith in the provisions of any present or future Swiss law.

6. The Bank shall be exempt and immune from all taxation included in the following categories:

(*a*) stamp, registration and other duties on all deeds or other documents relating to the incorporation or liquidation of the Bank;

(*b*) stamp and registration duties on any first issue of its shares by the Bank to a central bank, financial institution, banking group or underwriter at or before the time of incorporation or in pursuance of Article 7 or 9 of the Statutes;

(*c*) all taxes on the Bank's capital, reserves or profits, whether distributed or not, and whether assessed on the profits of the Bank before distribution or imposed at the time of distribution under the form of a coupon tax payable or deductible by the Bank. This provision is without prejudice to the State's right to tax the residents of Switzerland other than the Bank as it thinks fit;

(*d*) all taxes upon any agreements which the Bank may make in connection with the issue of loans for mobilising the German annuities and upon the bonds of such loans issued on a foreign market;

(*e*) all taxes on the remunerations and salaries paid by the Bank to members of its administration or its employees of non-Swiss nationality.

7. All funds deposited with the Bank by any Government in pursuance of the Plan adopted by The Hague Agreement of January, 1930, shall be exempt and immune from taxation whether by way of deduction by the Bank on behalf of the authority imposing the same or otherwise.

8. The foregoing exemptions and immunities shall apply to present and future taxation by whatsoever name it may be described, and whether imposed by the Confederation, or by the cantonal, communal or other public authorities.

9. Moreover, without prejudice to the exemptions specified above, there may not be levied on the Bank, its operation or its personnel any taxation other than that of a general character and to which other banking establishments established at Basle or in Switzerland, their operations and their personnel, are not subjected *de facto* and *de jure*.

10. The Bank, its property and assets and all deposits and other funds entrusted to it shall be immune in time of peace and in time of war from any measure such as expropriation, requisition, seizure, confiscation, prohibition or restriction

of gold or currency export or import, and any other similar measures.

11. Any dispute between the Swiss Government and the Bank as to the interpretation or application of the present Charter shall be referred to the Arbitral Tribunal provided for by The Hague Agreement of January, 1930.

The Swiss Government shall appoint a member to sit on the occasion of such dispute, the President having a casting vote.

In having recourse to the said Tribunal the Parties may nevertheless agree to submit their dispute to the President or to a member of the Tribunal chosen to act as sole Arbiter.

APPENDIX V

TRUST AGREEMENT

The following is the text of the Form of Trust Agreement between the Creditor Governments and the Bank for International Settlements. (Annex VIII. to The Hague Agreement.)

ENTERED into this   day of   1930, between the Governments of   et cetera (hereinafter called the Creditor Governments), of the one part, and the Bank for International Settlements (hereinafter called Trustee), of the second part,

     Witnesseth:

Whereas the Creditor Governments in connection with the carrying out of the New Plan as defined in The Hague Agreement of January, 1930 (hereinafter called the Plan), desire jointly to appoint the Bank for International Settlements their joint and sole trustee to receive, manage and distribute the annuities payable by Germany, and to perform other functions with respect thereto, all as provided by the Plan; and within the limits of the Statutes of the Bank;

Whereas the Bank for International Settlements has taken note of the provisions of the Plan and is prepared to accept the appointment as such trustee;

Therefore it is agreed between the parties hereto that the description, the conditions and the limitations of the functions of the Trustee with respect thereto and of the relations, obligations and rights of the parties are those set forth as follows:

Article 1

The Creditor Governments jointly appoint the Bank for International Settlements their joint and sole trustee for the purposes herein defined. The Bank accepts the appointment and agrees to carry out the trust on the conditions herein stated.

Article 2

The Trustee is empowered and agrees:

(*a*) To receive any balances transferred by the Agent General for Reparation Payments on the winding up of his accounts, subject to the rights of the different Creditor Governments in the distribution of such balances and to any claims and commitments thereon which may be outstanding at the time of transfer, all of which, as shown by the records of the Agent General for Reparation Payments, will be reported to the Trustee when the transfer is made;

(*b*) To hold in safe-keeping, as trustee, until the same shall be duly discharged, the Certificate of Debt, with coupons attached, issued and delivered by the German Government pursuant to the terms of the Plan, the receipt of which the Trustee acknowledges and a copy of which is attached hereto as Exhibit A;

(*c*) To hold in safe-keeping as trustee, until the same shall be duly discharged, the Certificate issued and delivered by the German Railway Company in acknowledgement of its liability, pursuant to the terms of the Plan, the receipt of which the Trustee acknowledges and a copy of which is attached hereto as Exhibit B;

(*d*) Commencing   1930, to receive in trust each month from the German Reich for the account of the Creditor Governments signatory hereto and for the account of the Trustees of the German External Loan 1924 all payments thereafter to be made by Germany under the Plan and the above-mentioned Certificate of Debt representing the service of the said Loan or the payment of the sums attributable to the said Creditor Governments on account of the non-postponable annuities and the postponable annuities as defined and specified in the Plan.

A certified Schedule stating the monthly and annual share during the whole period of the annuities of each Creditor

Government signatory hereto in the non-postponable and post-ponable portions and in the total of the German annuity is attached hereto as Exhibit C.

Article 3

Except during a period when the transfer of the postponable annuity is suspended, as provided for in Article 11 below, the Trustee will accept only currencies other than Reichsmarks in payment of the monthly instalments of the annuities payable by Germany, subject always to the proviso that the Trustee may accept Reichsmarks, in each month of a given annuity year, for an amount equal to one-twelfth of the total of any current annual programme for payments under Delivery in Kind and Reparation Recovery Act procedures for the year in question.

In arranging for the receipt of currencies other than Reichs-marks the Trustee, after having been notified of the require-ments of the Creditor Governments, will inform the German Government and, at the same time, the Reichsbank, at least one month in advance of the due dates for payment, of its pre-ferences relative to the currencies which it desires to have paid into its account. If these preferences are not complied with, the Trustee is authorised to accept payment from Germany entirely in the currencies of the creditor countries whose nationals were members of the Committee of Experts and as nearly as may be in proportion to the respective shares of these countries, it being understood that payments in currencies other than Reichsmarks which are not based upon the gold or gold exchange standard will only be made with the consent of the Trustee.

The Trustee will give receipts to the German Government for all sums which it pays or causes to be paid both on account of the postponable and on account of the non-postponable annuity. These receipts will show the currencies received as well as the equivalent value in Reichsmarks, with which the German Government will be credited.

At the end of each annuity year, when the Trustee has re-ceived from the German Government the sums due for that year, in accordance with the Plan, the Trustee shall surrender to the German Government the coupon of the Certificate of the German Government which corresponds to the payments of the year in question.

The Trustee takes note of the undertaking given by the German Government that the Reichsmark shall have and shall retain its convertibility in gold or foreign exchange as provided in Section 31 of the Law of the 30th August 1924, and that, in all circumstances, for the general purposes of the Plan, the Reichsmark shall have and shall retain a mint parity of 1/2790 kilogram of fine gold, as defined in the German coinage law of August 30, 1924.

The sums paid in currencies other than Reichsmarks into the annuity trust account shall be calculated in Reichsmarks, subject to the provisions of the above undertaking, at the average of the middle rates (Mittelkurs) prevailing on the Berlin Bourse during the period of fifteen days preceding the date of payment.

The sums in Reichsmarks paid by the German Railway Company to the account of the Trustee at the Reichsbank under the terms of the above-mentioned Certificate of Liability delivered by that Company, for an amount of fifty-five million Reichsmarks on the first day of each month in respect of the previous month, shall, until the due discharge of the Certificate, be placed each month at the disposal of the German Government by the Trustee as soon as they have been received, provided that the instalment of the Annuity payable by the German Government on the 15th day of the preceding month has been duly received.

Article 4

All the sums transferred from the account of the Agent-General for Reparations or paid on account of the German Annuities shall be received into an Annuity Trust Account. All the sums paid by Germany on account of the annuities shall be managed by the Trustee and shall be employed and distributed each month upon receipt as follows, on the understanding that the obligations of the Trustee in regard to the said sums shall be only those normally incumbent upon a banker for the execution of a trust agreement, and in no case shall the Trustee permit the accounts or credits of any Creditor Government to be overdrawn.

(a) In the first place, the sums required monthly for the service of the German External Loan, 1924, shall be transferred to the account or order of the Trustees of the said Loan, in conformity with the terms of the General Bond securing it, on the understanding that this appropriation shall have priority over all others. This service constitutes a first charge, expressly provided for as such, on the German annuities, whether non-postponable or postponable.

(b) One-twelfth of the share of each Creditor Government in the non-postponable Annuity shall be forthwith allocated in the books of the Trustee to that Government within the Annuity Trust Account in currencies other than reichsmarks. If one of the Governments has mobilised a part of the non-postponable annuity allotted to it, there shall be retained every month, out of the share due to that Government in virtue of the present paragraph, the sums required for the service of the obligations issued and outstanding, in conformity with the conditions of the contracts made on the occasion of such issues; these sums, deducted from the share of each of the Governments concerned in the issues, shall be transferred each month to a Trustee Account relating to the loan thus issued and shall remain there until the moment when payments have to be made for the interest service and amortisation of the obligations, in accordance with the terms of the respective loan agreements.

(c) One-twelfth of the share due to each Government for settling the quota of Deliveries in Kind allotted to it in a given year shall be forthwith allocated in the books of the Trustee to that Government within the Annuity Trust Account in Reichsmarks, if no other provision has been made by the Governments concerned, including Germany, for the settlement of this quota.

(d) One-twelfth of the sum due to each Government in each Annuity, after the allocations provided in paragraphs (b) and (c), shall be forthwith allocated in the books of the

Trustee to that Government within the Annuity Trust Account in currencies other than Reichsmarks.

(e) In application of Article 88 of the annexes to the Experts' Report of June 7, 1929 (hereinafter called the "Experts' Report"), the sums allocated as provided in the preceding paragraphs will remain without interest in the National Sub-Divisions of the Annuity Trust Account up to the equivalent of the following minimum amounts:

		Reichsmarks.
France	. . . .	68,037,500
Great Britain	. . .	26,587,500
Italy .	. . . .	13,887,500
Belgium	. . .	7,512,500
Roumania .	. . .	1,312,500
Jugoslavia .	. . .	5,462,500
Greece	. . .	450,000
Portugal	. . .	862,500
Japan .	. . .	862,500
Poland	. . .	25,000
		125,000,000 R.M.

All sums standing in the National Sub-Divisions of the Annuity Trust Account in excess of the above minimum non-interest-bearing deposits, may be freely withdrawn from the said account by the Creditor Governments, in accordance with the following paragraph.

(f) Subject to the foregoing and in accordance with the provisions of the Plan, the Trustee is authorised and agrees to transfer at such dates as may be indicated any sum allocated to any Government within the Annuity Trust Account to any interest-bearing account in the Bank for International Settlements or to any other bank or banker, or otherwise to dispose of it as the interested Creditor Government may direct; but in no case will the Trustee permit the accounts or credits of any Creditor Government to be overdrawn.

Article 5

The Trustee shall not be bound to pay any interest on balances in the Annuity Trust Account.

Article 6

Any exchange profit or loss arising from transactions carried out by the Trustee for account of Creditor Governments in connection with the management of the German annuities shall unless otherwise settled be credited or charged quarterly by the Trustee to the accounts of the Governments concerned, in proportion to their respective shares in the principal moneys involved, subject to the provisions of Article 4.

Article 7

The Trustee is authorised and agrees in connection with Delivery in Kind, Reparation Recovery Act, and other similar systems to pay in Reichsmarks up to the amount of the monthly Reichsmark balances available to the respective Creditor Governments on cheques, drafts or orders duly executed by the authorised representative of any such Creditor Government. The Creditor Governments respectively agree to keep the Trustee advised of the identity and authority of such representatives and to supply it with their specimen signatures.

Article 8

Payment by the Trustee in compliance with the documents referred to in the preceding article shall constitute full discharge to the Trustee for the Reichsmark payments made. Payments in currencies other than Reichsmarks made or transferred out of the Annuity Trust Account upon the order of a Creditor Government or effected under the authorisations contained in Article 4 above, shall constitute a full discharge to the Trustee for the payments made. In addition, as soon as possible after the close, of each annuity year when the respective Creditor Governments shall have received the annual account and auditor's report referred to in Article 17 hereof, the competent authority of each Creditor Government shall give the

Trustee a final global quittance and release for the actual payments made, during the Annuity year in question, to or upon the order of the Creditor Government concerned, as disclosed by the said accounts.

Article 9

The Trustee declares that it has taken note that the German Government undertakes during the period up to March 31, 1966, to maintain at the Bank a non-interest-bearing deposit equivalent to 50 per cent of the average deposit remaining in the Annuity Trust Account, but not exceeding 100 million Reichs marks.

The Bank shall to this end certify to the German Government and to the Creditor Governments every month the average of the balances at the close of each working day left by the Creditor Governments on deposit without interest during that month, in respect of the sums arising from the German payments under the Dawes Plan or under the present Plan up to the time when they are drawn out by the Creditor Governments.

The first deposit will be paid by the German Government to the Bank fifteen days after the coming into force of the New Plan, the amount of the deposit being calculated on the average of the daily balances above-mentioned left with the Agent-General or the Bank during the month ending two working days prior to the date of deposit, excluding sums returnable to the German Government under Annex III. of The Hague Protocol of August 31, 1929, or any supplementary arrangement. The deposit shall be maintained at the amount so calculated during one month. At the end of this period the deposit will be adjusted by a further deposit or by the withdrawal of part of the existing deposit on the basis of the average of the daily balances referred to above during the month ending two working days before the date of the adjustment. A similar adjustment will take place at the end of the second month from the date of the first deposit. At the end of the third month, and thereafter at intervals of three months, the deposit shall be adjusted on the basis of the average of the daily balances referred to above during the three months ending two working days before the date of each such adjustment. The intervals referred to in this paragraph may be changed by agreement between the Governments concerned with the concurrence of the Trustee.

The Trustee will accept this deposit under the conditions set out in this Article.

Article 10

The Trustee declares that it has taken note of the provisions of the Plan with respect to the functions assigned to the Bank of International Settlements in connection with any declaration of the German Government requiring the convening of the Special Advisory Committee, and the Trustee agrees and the Creditor Governments confirm that the Trustee shall carry out the functions assigned to it in that respect and in the manner described in the Plan.

The Trustee takes note that, in application of Article 124 of the Experts' Report, any recommendation of the Advisory Committee affecting the rights of the Creditor Governments shall not bind those Governments unless it is accepted and confirmed by the Creditor Governments which participated in the decision of September 16, 1928, to set up the Committee of Experts; and that similarly any recommendation affecting the rights of the German Government shall not bind that Government unless it is accepted and confirmed by that Government.

Article 11

Immediately on receiving from the German Government in conformity with the Plan notification of suspension of transfer of the whole or part of the postponable annuity the Trustee shall inform the Creditor Governments accordingly.

(*a*) As soon as this suspension becomes effective:

(1) The Trustee shall continue to transfer each month the sums necessary for assuring the service of the external loan of 1924 in accordance with paragraph (*a*) of Article 4 of this contract;

(2) The Trustee shall continue to credit or transfer each month in accordance with the provisions of paragraph (*b*) of

Article 4 of this Contract the sums paid by the German Government in respect of the non-postponable Annuity;

(3) In the event of a partial postponement, in any year, of transfer or of payment of the postponable annuities, the Trustee shall distribute the part of the postponable annuities actually paid and transferred in that year in such a manner as to ensure, so far as may be possible, that the receipts of the several Creditor Governments out of the aggregate payments actually transferred by Germany (whether on account of the unconditional or of the postponable annuities) shall be proportionate to their respective shares in the total annuities due by Germany under the Plan in respect of that year, provided always that the Creditor Governments entitled to an allocation out of the unconditional annuities shall in no case receive less than the allocations due to them respectively out of those annuities;

(4) Should the amount of the postponable annuities paid and transferred by Germany be insufficient to provide in full to each of the Creditor Governments its due share of the total German payments transferred, having regard to the allocations out of the unconditional annuity referred to in the previous paragraph, the Trustee shall, in accordance with the provisions of paragraph 202 of the Annexes to the Experts' Report, withdraw from the Guarantee Fund, to be constituted by the French Government, the sums necessary to make up the deficiency to each of the Creditor Governments concerned. The sums so withdrawn from the Guarantee Fund shall be repaid to that fund in accordance with the Plan at the end of the period of postponement.

(b) During the course of a partial or total postponement of transfer the Trustee may accept from Germany payments in Reichsmarks in respect of the amounts of which transfer has been postponed and of which payment has not been postponed under the Plan. The Trustee is authorised to give to the German Government receipts for such payments which will be in the nature of temporary acknowledgments. These acknowledgments will be converted into final receipts *pro tanto* on the transfer of the amounts postponed, or on the utilisation of the Reichsmarks accepted by the Trustee under this paragraph for payments in respect of deliveries in kind or in respect of Reparation Recovery Acts and similar procedures under the special programmes referred to in Annex IV. of the Experts' Report.

(c) Any sums accepted in Reichsmarks by the Trustee under paragraph (b) above will be distributed in the form of credits in the Trustee's books in such a way as to complete the credits due to each Creditor Government for the year in question under the Plan, and the Guarantee Fund in so far as it has been drawn upon. These Reichsmarks will be administered by the Trustee in the manner provided in the Plan.

(d) The parties to this contract agree that all investments of such Reichsmark funds effected by the Trustee shall be made for the individual account of the Creditor Governments, as their interests require, for their advantage and at their risk. In particular the proceeds of investment of Reichsmarks credited to the Guarantee Fund will be assigned to the French Government.

Article 12

The Creditor Governments and the Trustee agree that the Trustee shall have exclusive authority to act as agent of the Creditor Governments or any one of them, so far as concerns the operations relating to the mobilisation of the German Annuities, and that in the discharge of the functions and in the use of the authority entrusted to it as Agent in this matter, the Trustee will be guided by the provisions of the Plan which govern mobilisation. In particular the Trustee will abide by the following provisions:

(a) When it appears to the Trustee practically possible to proceed with an issue of Bonds representing the capitalisation of a part of the Annuity, the Trustee will inform the Creditor Governments. The possibility of proceeding with such an operation shall also be considered by the Trustee whenever so required by one or more of the Creditor Governments.

If after examination, and in cases other than that dealt with in the second part of paragraph (b) below, the Trustee considers such an operation inopportune, it shall indicate to the Governments concerned the reasons for this opinion.

(b) If one or more of the Governments concerned intend themselves to proceed in their own markets with an issue, the trustee shall fix the minimum conditions of issue at the time of the operation.

If, however, such an operation is intended in connection with internal conversion operations, the Government concerned will be free to offer the Bonds on its own market on whatever conditions it may be able to obtain, without its being necessary for the Trustee to consider whether the creation of the Bonds is opportune, and on the understanding that the Bonds will only be quoted on the market of issue.

(c) If one or more of the Governments concerned propose an international issue on other markets than their own respective markets, the Trustee shall at their request, if it considers on examination that conditions on these markets permit such an operation, take steps to proceed with this issue and determine, after making sure that the Central Banks concerned have no objection, the markets on which such offers may be made.

In the case of such issues, the various Governments having a share not yet mobilised in the non-postponable portion of the Annuity shall be given the right to participate in proportion to the following figures: France 500, Great Britain 84, Italy 42, Japan 6.6, Jugo-Slavia 6, Portugal 2.4.

No issue of an international character may however be made in the market of any of the countries the Government of which has signed this Trust Agreement without the approval of that Government both as regards the amount of the issue and as regards the conditions on which it shall be authorised.

(d) If it is decided to proceed with an issue, and if one or more of the Creditor Governments so request, the Trustee shall arrange, in agreement with those Governments and with the Issuing Bankers, the detailed conditions on which the Bonds shall be issued.

(e) The Trustee shall apply to the German Government, as provided in the Plan, for the creation of issuable Bonds.

(f) The Trustee declares its willingness to act as trustee or representative of the bondholders, or as agent for all issues of bonds made in pursuance of the provisions of the Plan relative to mobilisation, to the extent provided in the Loan Contract to be concluded between the Trustee and the Governments concerned on the occasion of an issue of such obligations.

(g) The expenses and commissions to be received by the Trustee both for the creation of bonds and for their issue shall be determined between the Trustee and the Governments concerned with regard to the importance of the functions which may be attributed to it on the occasion of each operation.

Article 13

The Trustee will credit to a special Trust Account the deposits which the French Government has undertaken to make, in the circumstances contemplated in the Plan, up to an amount of five hundred million Reichsmarks, in currencies other than Reichsmarks, based upon the gold or gold exchange standard.

The Trustee undertakes to administer these funds in such a way that the sums deposited shall be available in currencies other than Reichsmarks, based upon the gold or gold exchange standard, in order to equalise the short payments to the other Creditors during a period of transfer postponement.

Subject to the provisions of Article 11 (c) and (d), the Trustee will pay interest to the French Government, at the maximum current rate paid for long-term deposits, on the amount standing in this account in currencies other than Reichsmarks.

If it is agreed that this deposit shall remain for more than five years, the French Government shall be entitled to participate in the profits of the Bank in respect of this deposit on the terms laid down in Article 53 (e) (i) of its Statutes. It shall be restored to the French Government in the circumstances contemplated in the Plan.

Article 14

If the German Government elects to make the long term deposit up to four hundred million Reichsmarks, provided for in the Plan, the Trustee agrees to receive and administer this deposit and to take the consequent measures for allocation and utilisation of its profits according to the provision of Article 53 (*e*) of the Statutes of the Bank.

Article 15

In addition to making disbursements and keeping accounts in connection with Deliveries in Kind, Reparation Recovery Acts, and other similar systems as above provided, the Trustee declares that it takes note of the arrangements regarding Deliveries in Kind and Reparation Recovery Acts contained in the relevant Annexes to The Hague Agreement of January 1930, and agrees to observe the same as far as lies within its province and powers as a bank as set forth in the Statutes.

Article 16

The Trustee is authorised and agrees with respect to the assigned revenues of the Reich to exercise the discretions referred to in Section 3 of Annex III. of the Experts' Report.

Article 17

The Trustee shall furnish to each Creditor Government at the close of each month an account showing all the receipts and payments of the Trustee during that period in respect of the annuity received from Germany. The Trustee shall also furnish to each Creditor Government as soon as may be after the 31st March in the year 1931, and every succeeding year, a copy of the account as approved by the auditors of the Bank for International Settlements of all its operations in respect of the whole of the German Annuities, including the service of the German External Loan, 1924, since the close of the last preceding yearly account or, in the case of the first account, since the commencement of the operations of the Bank, and of any report that may be made by the Auditors on such accounts.

The Bank shall also furnish to each Creditor Government a copy of its Annual General Report as soon as published.

Article 18

From the date of coming into force of the present contract until its completion, the Creditor Governments, in addition to maintaining the deposits referred to in Article 4 (e), agree to pay to the Trustee a commission of 1 per mille on the actual payments received from the German Government on their behalf, in respect of the remuneration provided in Article 84 of the Annexes to the Experts' Report.

This payment will form a prior charge in favour of the Trustee, in accordance with the Plan, on the sums received by it on behalf of the Creditor Governments within the Annuity Trust Account.

The provisions of this Article will remain in force failing any new arrangement; such new arrangement may be made at the end of the first or of any one of the first five financial years, at the request of one of the signatory Powers or of the Trustee.

Article 19

The Trustee is authorised and agrees to notify forthwith to the Creditor Government any difficulty which may arise between it and the German Government relative to the interpretation or the application of the Plan.

Article 20

The Creditor Governments and the Trustee agree that, if any dispute shall arise between them or any of them with regard to the meaning or application of the provisions of this Trust Agreement, the dispute shall be referred for final decision to the Tribunal provided for by The Hague Agreement of January 1930, unless the parties to the dispute shall elect to refer the same to the President of the Tribunal or a member thereof selected as sole arbitrator.

Article 21

The present Contract shall come into force between the Trustee and the Creditor Governments whose representatives have signed it as soon as the Plan has been put into application and this Contract has been signed on behalf of the Trustee and of four of the following Powers: Belgium, France, Great Britain, Italy and Japan.

The French text is alone authentic.

APPENDIX VI

THE BANK AND THE HAGUE AGREEMENT

The following are extracts from the text of The Hague Agreement of January 1930:

Article 4

From and after the date on which the New Plan comes into force, the Office for Reparation Payments and the organisations in Berlin connected therewith shall be abolished and the relations with Germany of the Reparation Commission shall come to an end.

Under the regime of the New Plan only those of the functions of these organisations the maintenance of which is necessitated by the New Plan will continue in existence; these functions will be transferred to the Bank for International Settlements by the "Small Special Committee"; the Bank for International Settlements will exercise them within the conditions and limits of the New Plan in conformity with the provisions of its Statutes.

Article 6

The Contracting Parties recognise the necessity, with a view to putting into force the New Plan, of the constitution of the Bank for International Settlements. They recognise the corporate existence of the Bank to take effect as soon as it is constituted in accordance with the Statutes annexed to the law incorporating the Bank which is the subject of the Convention concluded with the Government of the Swiss Confederation.

Article 7

The Government of the Reich will deliver to the Bank for International Settlements, as Trustee for the Creditor Powers, the Debt Certificate referred to in Annex III.

Further, the German Government guarantees that the German Railway Company (Deutsche Reichsbahngesellschaft) will deliver to the Bank for International Settlements the Certificate mentioned in Annex IV.

Article 10

The Contracting Parties will take in their respective territories the measures necessary for securing that the funds and investments of the Bank, resulting from the payments by Germany, shall be freed from all national or local fiscal charges.

The Bank, its property and assets, and also the deposits of other funds entrusted to it, on the territory of, or dependent on the administration of, the Parties shall be immune from any disabilities and from any restrictive measures such as censorship, requisition, seizure or confiscation, in time of peace or war, reprisals, prohibition or restriction of export of gold or currency and other similar interferences, restrictions or prohibitions.

Article 11

The Governments of the Creditor Powers have settled the text of a Trust Agreement, appearing in Annex VIII., for the receipt, management and division of the German annuities.

The Bank for International Settlements upon its establishment will be invited to give its adhesion to the Agreement, and the Governments referred to will appoint Delegates with the powers necessary to sign.

The German Government declares that it has been informed of the text of the Agreement.

Article 15

1. Any dispute, whether between the Governments signatory to the present Agreement or between one or more of those Governments and the Bank for International Settlements, as

to the interpretation or application of the New Plan shall, subject to the special provisions of Annexes I., V.a, VI.a and IX. be submitted for final decision to an arbitration tribunal of five members appointed for five years, of whom one, who will be the Chairman, shall be a citizen of the United States of America, two shall be nationals of States which were neutral during the late war; the two other shall be respectively a national of Germany and a national of one of the Powers which are creditors of Germany.

For the first period of five years from the date when the New Plan takes effect this Tribunal shall consist of the five members who at present constitute the Arbitration Tribunal established by the Agreement of London of the 30th August 1924.

2. Vacancies on the Tribunal, whether they result from the expiration of the five-yearly periods or occur during the course of any such period, shall be filled, in the case of a member who is a national of one of the Powers which are creditors of Germany, by the French Government, which will first reach an understanding for this purpose with the Belgian, British, Italian and Japanese Governments; in the case of the member of German nationality, by the German Government; and in the cases of the three other members by the six Governments previously mentioned acting in agreement, or in default of their agreement, by the President for the time being of the Permanent Court of International Justice.

3. In any case in which either Germany or the Bank is plaintiff or defendant, if the Chairman of the Tribunal considers, at the request of one or more of the Creditor Governments parties to the proceedings, that the said Government or Governments are principally concerned, he will invite the said Government or Governments to appoint—and in the case of more Governments than one, by agreement—a member, who will take the place on the Tribunal of the member appointed by the French Government.

In any case in which, on the occasion of a dispute between two or more Creditor Governments, there is no national of one or more of those Governments among the Members of the Tribunal, that Government or those Governments shall have

P

the right to appoint each a Member who will sit on that occasion. If the Chairman considers that some of the said Governments have a common interest in the dispute, he will invite them to appoint a single member. Whenever, as a result of this provision, the Tribunal is composed of an even number of members, the Chairman shall have a casting vote.

4. Before and without prejudice to a final decision, the Chairman of the Tribunal, or, if he is not available in any case, any other Member appointed by him, shall be entitled, on the request of any Party who makes the application, to make any interlocutory order with a view to preventing any violation of the rights of the Parties.

5. In any proceedings before the Tribunal the Parties shall always be at liberty to agree to submit the point at issue to the Chairman or any one of the Members of the Tribunal chosen as a single arbitrator.

6. Subject to any special provisions which may be made in the Submission—provisions which may not in any event affect the right of intervention of a Third Party—the procedure before the Tribunal or a single arbitrator shall be governed by the rules laid down in Annex XII.

The same rules, subject to the same reservation, shall also apply to any proceedings before this Tribunal for which the Annexes to the present Agreement provide.

7. In the absence of an understanding on the terms of Submission, any Party may seize the Tribunal directly by a proceeding *ex parte*, and the Tribunal may decide, even in default of appearance, any question of which it is thus seized.

8. The Tribunal, or the single arbitrator, may decide the question of their own jurisdiction, provided always that, if the dispute is one between Governments and a question of jurisdiction is raised, it shall, at the request of either Party, be referred to the Permanent Court of International Justice.

9. The present provisions shall be duly accepted by the Bank for the settlement of any dispute which may arise between it and one or more of the signatory Governments as to the interpretation or application of its Statutes or the New Plan.

Final Clause

The New Plan will come into force and will be considered as having been put into execution on the date on which the Reparation Commission and the Chairman of the Kriegslastenkommission have agreed in reporting:

(1) The ratification of the present Agreement by Germany and the enactment of the German laws in accordance with the relative Annexes.

(2) The ratification of the present Agreement by four of the following Powers, that is to say, Belgium, Great Britain, France, Italy and Japan.

(3) The constitution of the Bank for International Settlements and the acceptance by the Bank of the undertakings by it for which the present Agreement provides, and also its receipt of the Certificate of the German Government and the Certificate of the German Railway Company as provided in Annexes III. and IV.

APPENDIX VII

THE BANK AND THE GERMAN REPARATION DEBT

The following are extracts from Annex III. of The Hague Agreement:

ANNEX III

DEBT CERTIFICATE OF THE GERMAN GOVERNMENT

I

The German Government, by this present Certificate, undertakes a solemn engagement subject to the stipulations of the New Plan as defined by Article 1 of the Agreement of The Hague of January 1930, to pay to the Bank for International Settlements as Trustee for the Creditor Powers, and not to any other agent nor by way of direct payment to any one of its creditors, and in conformity with the following provisions, the annuities set out in the following table plus the sums required for the service of the German External Loan, 1924, as provided in the General Bond dated October 10, 1924.

II

1. Except for any period in which the transfer of the postponable portion of the annuity is suspended, the monthly payments of the Reich must be made in currencies other than the Reichsmark.

2. Provided always that with a view to the execution of the programmes relating to deliveries in kind and of the arrangements under the Reparation Recovery Acts, and with a view

to meeting any administrative expenses incurred in Germany, the Bank of International Settlements may request that a corresponding part of these payments may be made in Reichsmarks.

3. The Bank may notify to the German Government and the Reichsbank simultaneously one month at least in advance of the payment dates the Bank's preferences with respect to the currencies in which payment is to be made. In case these preferences are not complied with, the Government of the Reich may make payment of such parts of the German annuities as do not relate to the service of the German External Loan, 1924, in the currencies of the Creditor countries whose nationals were members of the Committee of Experts of 1929, divided as nearly as possible in proportion to their respective shares, it being, however, understood that payments in currencies other than the Reichsmark which are not on a gold or gold exchange standard shall be made only with the consent of the Bank.

4. The Bank for International Settlements shall give its receipt to the German Government for all sums which it pays or causes to be paid under this Certificate. The receipt shall make note of the currencies received, but credit shall be given to the German Government in the Reichsmark equivalent of these currencies.

The Bank's receipt giving credit in Reichsmarks for payments made to the Bank for International Settlements by the German Government or on its behalf for the execution of the New Plan, shall during the normal operation of the New Plan constitute a complete and sufficient discharge of the obligations of the German Government with respect to such payments.

Should, however, transfer postponement be in whole or partial effect, the Bank's receipt giving credit in Reichsmarks shall constitute a complete and sufficient discharge of the obligations of the German Government with respect to all payments into the Annuity Trust Account made in foreign exchange and with respect to such portions of the payments made in Reichsmarks as in the opinion of the Bank provide current funds for deliveries in kind or services. As to the remainder, the receipt of the Bank shall be in the nature of a temporary acknowledgment only.

5. The German Government undertakes that the Reichsmark shall have and retain its convertibility into gold or devisen as contemplated in Section 31 of the Reichsbank Law of the 30th August 1924, and that in all circumstances for the general purposes of the New Plan the Reichsmark shall have and shall retain a mint parity of 1/2790 kilogramme of fine gold as defined in the German Coinage Law of the 30th August 1924.

Sums paid in currencies other than Reichsmarks into the Annuity Trust Account shall be calculated in terms of Reichsmarks subject to the provisions of the last preceding paragraph at the average of the middle rates (Mittelkurs) prevailing on the Berlin Bourse during the fifteen days preceding the date of payment.

III

1. To this Certificate are attached coupons representing each the whole of one annuity payable, after deduction of the amounts required for the service of the German External Loan, 1924; each coupon is divided into two parts—Part A represents that part of the annuity which is mobilisable and non-postponable; Part B the postponable portion of each annuity. Each part of the annuity coupon enjoys absolutely equal rights throughout except with regard to the possibility of postponement hereinafter provided for.

2. The Bank shall distribute moneys in payment of the mobilised or mobilisable portions of the annuity coupon among the whole of the bondholders and the Creditor Governments in proportion to the rights of each to share in the portion of the annuity coupons not subject to postponement, without allowing a priority of any kind to any tranche or to any claim. It will distribute the moneys relating to the non-mobilisable portions of the annuity coupons amongst the Creditor Governments, the transfer of these moneys taking place only after the transfer of the moneys relating to the mobilised or mobilisable portion of the annuity coupon.

IV

1. The service of interest and amortisation of the mobilisable or mobilised portions of the annuity coupons shall be paid to the Bank in currencies other than the Reichsmark by the German Reich without any reservation, *i.e.* on its own responsibility. The financial service of these mobilisable or mobilised portions of the annuities shall constitute a final and unconditional international obligation in the ordinary financial sense of the word.

2. Furthermore, upon the request of the Bank for International Settlements, acting as trustee of the Creditor Powers, if and in so far as the Bank considers such a course opportune, Germany undertakes to substitute for Part A of the coupons issuable bonds bearing its name, representing, on the same conditions as this Certificate and the said coupons, an obligation of the Reich. The amount and form of these bonds and the specifications of the currency in which they shall be issued shall be fixed by the Bank.

3. If any one or more of the Creditor States should intend to utilise internal issues of German bonds in connection with operations for the conversion of national debt, such bonds shall be quoted only on their market of issue.

4. If and in so far as Germany shall redeem reparation loans (general or conversion loans) which can be redeemed before their due date according to the issue conditions, the part of the annuity destined for the service of the loan so redeemed will accrue to Germany. It is understood that the Bank will, as far as possible, make every effort to secure that loans will not be issued without granting to Germany an appropriate right of anticipated redemption.

5. Germany shall have the right to redeem all or any part of the not yet mobilised annuities (Parts A and B of the coupons) on a basis of $5\frac{1}{2}$ per cent. discount.

V

1. The payment of the non-mobilisable portion of the annuity coupons shall be made to the Bank for International Settle-

ments by the German Government in the same conditions as that of the mobilised or mobilisable portion of the annuity coupons.

6. Any sum in Reichsmarks the transfer of which is postponed shall be deposited to the account of the Bank for International Settlements at the Reichbank for eventual release of balances not absorbed by deliveries in kind, against payments in foreign currencies by the German Government. At all times the employment, whether for investment or for deliveries in kind, of Reichsmarks so deposited shall be subject to agreement between the Reichsbank and the Bank for International Settlements.

9. At the end of any period in respect of which a total or partial postponement of transfer or payment has been declared for any monthly instalment, the instalment or part thereof the transfer or payment of which has been so postponed shall become immediately payable to the Bank for International Settlements in foreign currencies, with the exception of any amounts of which the Creditor Powers have already had the benefit in some other form in pursuance of the New Plan. This clause modifies in no way the functions of the Special Advisory Committee provided for in the New Plan.

10. In the event of any declaration of postponement made by Germany or at any other time when the German Government declares to the Creditor Governments and to the Bank for International Settlements, that it has come to the conclusion in good faith that Germany's exchange and economic life may be seriously endangered by the transfer in part or in full of the postponable portion of the annuities, the Bank for International Settlements shall convene the Special Advisory Committee mentioned in Chapter 8 (e) of the Experts' Plan of the 7th June 1929.

The Special Advisory Committee shall forthwith consider the situation in all its aspects, as provided in the Plan, and shall indicate for consideration by the Governments and the Bank what, in their opinion, are the measures that should be taken in regard to the application of the Plan. In application of Article 124 of the Report of the Experts of the 7th June 1929, any recommendation of the Committee affecting the rights of the Creditor Governments shall not bind the Creditor Govern-

ments unless it is accepted and confirmed by the Creditor
Governments who participated in the decision of September
16, 1928, to set up the Committee of Experts. Similarly, any recommendation affecting the rights of the German Government
shall not bind the German Government unless it is accepted
and confirmed by that Government.

VI

The German Government undertakes during the period up
to March 31, 1966, to maintain at the Bank for International
Settlements a non-interest bearing deposit equivalent to 50
per cent of the average deposit remaining in the Annuity Trust
Account, but not exceeding 100 million Reichsmarks.

The Bank shall to this end certify to the German Government
and to the Creditor Governments every month the average of
the balance at the close of each working day left by the Creditor
Governments on deposit without interest during that month,
in respect of the sums arising from the German payments under
the Dawes Plan or under the New Plan up to the time when
they are drawn out by the Creditor Governments.

The first deposit will be paid by the German Government
to the Bank fifteen days after the putting into execution of
the New Plan, the amount of the deposit being calculated on
the average of the daily balances above mentioned left with the
Agent-General for Reparation Payments or the Bank during the
month ending two working days prior to the date of deposit,
excluding sums returnable to the German Government under
Annex III. of The Hague Protocol of August 31, 1929.

The deposit shall be maintained at the amount so calculated
during one month. At the end of this period the deposit will be
adjusted by a further deposit or by the withdrawal of part of
the existing deposit, on the basis of the average of the daily
balances referred to above during the month ending two working days before the date of the adjustment.

A similar adjustment will take place at the end of the second
month from the date of the first deposit.

At the end of the third month, and thereafter, at intervals of
three months, the deposit shall be adjusted on the basis of the

average of the daily balances referred to above during the three months ending two working days before the date of each such adjustment. The interval referred to in this paragraph may be changed by agreement between the Governments concerned with the concurrence of the Bank for International Settlements.

VIII

The obligation of the German Government in relation to the annuities for which this Certificate provides shall not be deemed to have been fulfilled until all sums, the transfer or payment of which may from time to time have been suspended, have been either in fact completely transferred to the Bank for International Settlements in the shape of approved currency other than the Reichsmark or employed for deliveries in kind.

IX

At the end of each annuity period, when the Bank for International Settlements has received from the German Government the amounts due under this present Certificate, the Bank will return to the Government the coupon corresponding to the payments of that annuity period. The Certificate itself will be delivered when all the coupons have been paid.

ANNUITY COUPON (NOT INCLUDING THE SERVICE OF THE GERMAN EXTERNAL LOAN, 1924)

Part A

The German Reich will pay to the Creditor Powers at the Bank for International Settlements on account of the non-postponable part of the Annuity for the period from the   , 19 , to the   , 19 , the sum of 612,000,000 Reichsmarks.

The relative provisions of

Part B

The German Reich will pay to the Creditor Powers at the Bank for International Settlements on account of the postponable part of the Annuity for the period from the   , 19 , to the   19 , the sum of Reichsmarks.

The relative provisions of

the Certificate apply to the
present coupon.

A note of the payment of
each instalment will be endorsed on the present coupon.
When the full amount of the
above sum has been paid this
coupon will be returned to the
German Government.

Berlin, the   , 1930.
Reichsschuldenverwaltung.
(Administration of the Debt
of the Reich.)

the Certificate apply to the
present coupon.

A note of the payment of
each instalment will be endorsed on the present coupon.
When the full amount of the
above sum has been paid this
coupon will be returned to the
German Government.

Berlin, the   , 1930.
Reichsschuldenverwaltung.
(Administration of the Debt
of the Reich.)

APPENDIX VIII

THE BANK AND THE GERMAN BANK LAW

*The following are extracts from Annexes V. and V.A of The Hague
Agreement:*

ANNEX V

PROVISIONS TO BE INSERTED OR MAINTAINED IN THE GERMAN BANK LAW

Article 21

Add at end as new paragraph:

"All functions confided to and obligations imposed on
Central Banks in general or any one such Central Bank
specially by the New Plan (Hague Agreement, January 1930)
will be performed in Germany by the Reichsbank. All functions confided to and obligations imposed on Presidents of
Central Banks in general or any one such President specially
by the New Plan will be performed in Germany by the President of the Reichsbank."

ANNEX V.A

PROCEDURE FOR THE MODIFICATION OF CERTAIN PROVISIONS OF THE GERMAN BANK LAW

Any proposal which may affect the provisions of Annex V.
must be submitted by the German Government to the Board
of Directors of the Bank for International Settlements.

The Board may object to any such proposal, on the ground
that it is incompatible with the New Plan, by referring the

question within a period of two months, in the absence of an agreement being reached, to an arbitrator chosen by common consent, or, in default of such consent, to the Tribunal provided for in the present Agreement. The decision of the arbitrator or Tribunal shall be final and will bind the Reich, the Bank for International Settlements and the States signatory to the present Agreement.

APPENDIX IX

THE BANK AND THE GERMAN RAILWAY LAW

The following are extracts from Annex VI. of The Hague Agreement:

ANNEX VI

AMENDMENTS TO BE MADE IN THE LAW AND IN THE STATUTES CONCERNING THE GERMAN RAILWAY COMPANY

Section 4.— REPARATION TAX

(1) The Company shall pay, as a contribution of the Deutsche Reichsbahn to the reparation annuities payable by the Reich, a tax of the Reich to an amount of 660 million Reichsmarks per annum (reparation tax). The reparation tax shall fall due, in equal monthly instalments of 55 million Reichsmarks, upon expiration of each month on the first day of each subsequent month, and where the first day is a Sunday or holiday, upon the first working day following; the tax shall be paid direct into the account of the Bank for International Settlements at the Reichsbank; the first payment shall fall due on the 1st October 1929, and the last payment on the 1st April 1966, subject to the provision of Section 5 of the present Law. The payments shall be made before 9 A.M. on the days fixed for the same.

(3) The Company shall deposit with the Bank for International Settlements a certificate acknowledging its liabilities under paragraphs (1) and (2) above. The Reparation Bonds created in virtue of Section 4 of the Law of the 30th August 1924, and handed over to the Trustee, shall be cancelled and destroyed in the presence of a representative of the Company.

(4) The payment of the reparation tax by the Company shall be guaranteed by the Government of the Reich. As soon as the Bank for International Settlements notifies the Government that a payment due has not been effected either in whole or in part, the Government shall authorise the Company to devote to the payment of the arrears of reparation tax the proceeds of the transport tax collected for the account of the Reich, in so far as such a tax exists. If these resources prove insufficient the Reich shall meet the deficit within one month of receiving notice from the Bank, either by placing the sums required for the payment at the disposal of the Company or by making a direct payment into the account of the Bank for International Settlements at the Reichsbank. Apart from the above provision, the transport tax shall be exempt from all special charges in respect of reparations.

(5) The sums paid by the Government to cover a deficit in the reparation tax and the proceeds of the transport tax devoted by the Company to the same purpose in virtue of paragraph (4) above shall be repaid to the Reich in conformity with the provisions of Section 25, paragraph (3), No. 3 of the Company's Statutes.

(6) The Company is entitled, with the assent of the Bank for International Settlements and subject to the terms agreed on with the Bank, to discharge the reparation tax in whole or in part by a capital payment. The Government of the Reich may require the Company to exercise this right of discharge provided that the Reich places the necessary funds at the Company's disposal. Any capital payment shall extinguish the liability of the Company under paragraphs (1) and (2) in a corresponding degree. The right of the Government of the Reich provided for in the Agreement of   of
relating to the redemption of reparation annuities remains unaffected.

Section 5.—CONCESSIONS. TRANSFER OF RIGHTS AND OBLIGATIONS

(2) In the event of the Company's liability to pay the reparation tax direct into the account of the Bank for Interna-

tional Settlements at the Reichsbank terminating before the
31st December 1964, the concession shall be shortened accordingly and will terminate forthwith, provided that the preference shares have all been redeemed by that date. On the
other hand, if at the 31st December 1964, the whole of the
Reparation tax payments due up to that date have not been
made, or if the whole of the preference shares have not been
redeemed, the concession shall be prolonged under the same
conditions until such time as the payment of the tax and the
redemption of the preference shares have been completed.

APPENDIX X

THE BANK AND GERMAN ASSIGNED REVENUES

The following are extracts from Annex VII. of The Hague Agreement:

ANNEX VII

ASSIGNMENT BY WAY OF COLLATERAL GUARANTEE OF CERTAIN REVENUES OF THE GERMAN GOVERNMENT

1. The German Government assigns, subject to the charge in favour of the Trustees for the German External Loan, 1924, the proceeds of the Customs, of the tobacco taxes, the beer tax and the tax on spirits (Administration of the Monopoly) for the service of the certificate representing the annuities payable by Germany, including the service of any bonds which may be issued under the provisions of the New Plan. To this end, the Reich, without prejudice to its general responsibility for the payment of the annuities and its entire discretion to effect these payments out of general revenues, will secure out of the receipts from the above revenues by way of collateral guarantee the sums necessary to cover the annuities as elsewhere determined. The assignment constitutes a negative pledge and is ruled by the following conditions:

2. The Reich will not create any charge on the assigned revenues for any other loan or credit without the consent of the Bank for International Settlements. If any such charge is created on the assigned revenues with the consent of the Bank, the charge for the annuities payable by Germany will rank ahead of any such other charge.

3. If at any time the total yield of the assigned revenues should fall below 150 per cent. of the highest budgetary contribution payable by Germany under the New Plan, the Bank may require that additional revenues sufficient to assure the immediate restoration of the yield to the above percentage be assigned and the German Government will forthwith comply with that requirement accordingly.

4. Should the German Government change the system of collecting any of the assigned revenues, then the receipts secured to the Reich by the new system will be assigned in substitution for the original tax.

APPENDIX XI

THE BANK AND DELIVERIES IN KIND

The following are extracts from Annex IX. of The Hague Agreement:

ANNEX IX

REGULATIONS FOR DELIVERIES IN KIND

Article 4

Organisation

17. The management of deliveries in kind includes two separate parts, namely, the approval of contracts and the handling of the funds reserved for deliveries in kind. The creditor Governments concerned and the German Government remain responsible for the approval of contracts and entrust the management of the funds reserved for deliveries in kind to the Bank for International Settlements.

18. A contract is approved if there is agreement with regard to it between the creditor Government concerned and the German Government.

19. Each creditor Government concerned in deliveries in kind and the German Government shall appoint an agent, whose duty it shall be to deal with all matters concerning deliveries in kind and to fulfil all functions devolving upon him under the present Regulations.

Each agent shall remain responsible to his Government for the strict application of the provisions of these Regulations.

The agents of the German, Belgian, British, French, Italian,

Japanese and Yugo-Slav Governments shall assemble whenever a Government concerned in deliveries in kind considers
a meeting to be necessary. The meeting shall be called by the
agent of the Government which proposes it.

The same agents shall meet every year, in principle during
the second fortnight in May, in order to review the general
situation as shown by the statistical documents supplied by the
Bank for International Settlements.

20. The agent of the German Government will be in permanent residence at Paris, where the agents will meet in all the
cases for which provision is made in the present Regulations.
The agents of the Creditor Powers are under no obligation to
have a fixed place of residence.

21. The Bank for International Settlements can incur no
responsibility except with regard to the duties arising from the
mandate with which it is entrusted.

22. The Bank for International Settlements will effect the
payments to be made in virtue of duly approved contracts
which are transmitted to it by the agent of the German Government or are sent by the agent of the Creditor Power concerned
in execution of a decision of the arbitrator in virtue of Article 7
hereafter.

23. The Bank will keep all accounts and statistics, and will
exercise all supervision in respect of these payments.

24. The Bank is also at liberty, in accordance with paragraph 28 of Annex 1. to the Experts' Plan of the 7th June 1929,
to appoint an Advisory Committee, the object of which would
be to inform generally the Bank of the progress of deliveries in
kind.

This Committee may, if it thinks fit, convoke those agents of
the Governments who do not form part of the Committee.

.   .   .   .

57. Within three clear working days of receiving the contract the agent of the German Government shall inform the
agent which has transmitted the contract whether he accepts
it with or without reservation or whether he proposes its rejection.

58. If he has no objection to the contract he will inform the

Bank for International Settlements, to which he will send a copy of the contract.

.   .   .   .

63. When an appeal is made to the arbitrator the award shall be notified to the German agent and the agent of the Creditor Power concerned. The latter may then send the contract direct to the Bank for International Settlements, and shall be responsible for informing the German agent to this effect.

64. When a contract does not provide a definite scheme of payments the German agent will draw up a schedule in agreement with the agent or authorised department of the creditor Government, in order that the Bank for International Settlements may set aside the sums required for paying for the contract.

65. The Bank for International Settlements will keep accounts for each creditor country showing the dates and amounts of the payments for which the approved contracts provide and indicating how much of the quota remains available for new contracts.

Abstracts of these accounts will be supplied on the 1st and the 15th of each month to the agent of the Creditor Power concerned and to the German agent.

66. Before submitting a contract for approval the creditor Government concerned shall have definitely agreed with the purchaser the terms on which he can obtain payments out of the funds reserved for deliveries in kind.

67. If, in the course of execution of a contract, the buyer does not fulfil these conditions he shall continue to bear the entire responsibility for the contract, as far as the seller is concerned, under ordinary commercial conditions, even if the contract stipulates that it shall only be executed as a delivery in kind.

68. In this case the Bank for International Settlements shall, if the Creditor Power concerned so requests, on its own responsibility release the credits reserved but not yet utilised for payment for the contract.

72. In transmitting to the Bank for International Settle-

ments a contract in respect of which exceptions have been admitted in application of paragraphs 69, 70 and 71, the agent of the German Government shall attach to the contract a note stating the nature of the exception granted and indicating which agents have given their consent.

In the case of contracts approved in virtue of an arbitral decision in accordance with paragraph 63, the agent who transmits the contract will attach to it a copy of the arbitral decision.

73. The statistics which the Bank for International Settlements will keep in execution of paragraph 23 will be sent by the Bank each month to the agents of all the Governments and will show:

(1) according to countries and categories the total amount of the contracts which it has received during the preceding month, those for an amount exceeding 5 million reichsmarks and riders thereto being shown separately;

(2) the information transmitted to it with contracts in accordance with paragraph 72.

Article 8

Payments

(A.)—*Payments for Deliveries in Kind.*

74. For each Creditor Government there shall be opened at the Bank for International Settlements an account to which shall be credited all sums to be reserved by that Government for deliveries in kind according to the approved schedule. All payments made in respect of approved contracts shall be debited to this account.

75. The credit balance at the end of each month shall be added to the credits opened during the following month. The sum available to the Creditor Power for deliveries in kind during that month shall be the total of these two amounts.

76. At the beginning of each month the agent of the creditor Government concerned and the agent of the German Government shall be informed of the state of the account.

77. Subject to the reserves provided by the present Regulations the sums paid to this account can only be employed for the payment of contracts for deliveries in kind.

78. For the purpose of paying for duly approved contracts for deliveries in kind each Creditor Power may dispose freely of the credit balance lying in his account, by any method of payment which is current in international commerce, and particularly by means of cheques, orders to transfer and time drafts.

The payments will be made by the Reichsbank in Berlin.

79. The Creditor Powers will transmit to the Bank for International Settlements the names and signatures of the officials who are authorised to issue orders to pay.

80. In principle, orders to pay shall be made out in Reichsmarks. When a contract stipulates that payment is to be made in a non-German currency, the order to pay shall be made out in this currency, but must bear the inscription: "Payable in Reichsmarks". In this case the conversion into Reichsmarks shall be made at the time of payment, at the official average rate of the Berlin Bourse as quoted for the day preceding that of payment.

81. If a contract provides for an agreed rate of conversion, the conversion into Reichsmarks shall be made at this rate.

82. All orders to pay must indicate the approval number of the contract in respect of which they are issued.

83. Cheques shall be issued by the Creditor Government made out in the name of the seller and passed to the buyer for transmission to the seller. They cannot be cashed over the counter, but must be passed through a bank account.

84. Orders to transfer shall bear the names of the buyer and seller, as well as that of the bank responsible for collection.

85. Time drafts shall be made payable not less than thirty days and not more than ninety days at most from the date of issue. They shall only be issued if the contract for which they are required makes provision to this effect.

They shall be drawn by the Creditor Government on the Bank for International Settlements. They shall not be accepted.

They shall be issued to the order of the buyer, who shall endorse them and transmit them direct to the seller.

They shall bear the words: "Payable at the Reichsbank in Berlin."

86. If a Creditor Government which has issued a time draft does not possess credits sufficient to meet the payment when it falls due, it shall place the necessary funds at the disposal of the Bank for International Settlements two days before the due date.

A Creditor Government which advances a sum in this manner shall be reimbursed out of the first credits which are thereafter placed at its disposal for deliveries in kind.

87. The issuing Authority and the agent of the German Government will receive daily advice and periodical statements of the payments effected.

88. The rules to be applied to the payments made in application of the preceding paragraphs will be determined jointly by representatives of the German, Belgian, British, French, Italian, Japanese and Yugo-Slav Governments and the Bank for International Settlements, particularly in so far as concerns the requisite measures for safeguarding these payments.

89. When a seller has to make a payment to a buyer in executing or winding-up a contract the buyer shall inform his Government and request the seller to make the payment into the account for deliveries in kind opened for this Government.

90. This provision shall not apply to any payments of less than 10,000 Reichsmarks and of less than 20 per cent of the value of the contract, which the seller may be liable to make to the purchaser after the last payment for which the contract provides has been made and the contract is consequently regarded by the contracting parties as terminated. In such a case the payments shall be made by the seller direct to the purchaser.

(B.)—*Direct Payments.*

91. When the case arises the provisions of Article 6 of the present Regulations concerning the direct payment of a part of the value of certain commodities or services shall be applied to a contract either:

(*a*) by the terms of the contract itself, or

(*b*) by the decision concerning the approval of the contract, such decision being regarded as conditional within the meaning of Article 7.

In the first case the dates and amounts of the sums to be paid direct shall be stipulated in the contract.

In the second case the dates and amounts of the sums to be paid direct shall be fixed by the decision of approval in such a manner that the direct payments are made at the same time and in the same proportions as the payments made on account of deliveries in kind.

In both cases the purchaser shall make the direct payments to the seller in accordance with the rules of ordinary commerce.

92. The foregoing provisions shall not preclude the Bank for International Settlements in agreement with the Creditor Power concerned from meeting all the payments for which a contract provides, when they fall due. In this case the direct payments shall be made under the conditions and in the currencies stipulated in the contract, but it shall be debited to the Creditor Power in an account other than that relating to deliveries in kind.

Article 10

Infractions and Frauds

99. The Bank for International Settlements shall not incur any responsibility by reason of any fraud or irregularity committed during the execution of a contract. But it shall inform the agent of the Creditor Government concerned and the German agent of any fact which may appear to it to constitute a fraud or wilful infraction of the present Regulations.

105. If before the last payment under a contract has been made, the buyer or seller is found guilty by his Government of fraud or wilful infraction of the present Regulations, and if his name is notified in accordance with paragraph 102, no further payment shall be made out of the funds for deliveries in kind in respect of the contract, which shall be liquidated direct between buyer and seller.

If the sums paid up to that time exceed the value of the

commodities or services due to be delivered under the contract, the Governments concerned shall do their utmost to obtain repayment of the excess to the account for deliveries in kind of the Creditor Power.

106. In order that the provisions of the preceding paragraph may be applied, the agent of the Power which has declared its national to be excluded shall inform the Bank for International Settlements of the measures taken in this respect.

APPENDIX XII

THE BANK AND THE REPARATION RECOVERY ACT

The following are extracts from Annexes X. and X.A of The Hague Agreement:

ANNEX X

AGREEMENT FOR AMENDING THE METHOD OF ADMINISTERING "THE GERMAN REPARATION (RECOVERY) ACT, 1921"

I

The German Government undertake to pay each month on the same dates as the other payments forming the postponable annuity to the Bank for International Settlements for the account of His Britannic Majesty's Government the sterling equivalent of the Reichsmark sums available under the New Plan for transfer by means of the Reparation (Recovery) Act to His Britannic Majesty's Government, provided always that the amounts so paid shall not exceed twenty-six per cent. of the sterling value of the German goods imported into Great Britain during the preceding month but one.

ANNEX X.A

(Translation.)

AGREEMENT REGARDING THE METHOD OF ADMINISTERING THE LEVY ON THE VALUE OF GERMAN IMPORTS INTO FRANCE

I

The German Government undertake to pay each month on the same dates as the other payments forming the postponable annuity to the Bank of International Settlements for the account of the French Government the equivalent in French francs of the Reichsmark sums available under the New Plan for transfer to the French Government by means of the levy on the value of German imports into France, provided always that the amounts so paid shall not exceed twenty-six per cent. of the value in francs of the German goods imported into France and Algeria during the preceding month but one.

APPENDIX XIII

THE BANK AND THE MOBILISATION OF GERMAN ANNUITIES

The following are extracts from the "Agreement as to the Financial Mobilisation of German Annuities" concluded at The Hague in January 1930:

ARRANGEMENT AS TO THE FINANCIAL MOBILISATION OF THE GERMAN ANNUITIES

2. The German Government declares that it will not issue any external long term loan before the 1st October 1930, or, if the issue referred to in the preceding paragraph has not taken place before this date, before the expiry of one year from the date of the delivery to the Bank for International Settlements of the Debt Certificate of the Reich, on the understanding that this undertaking shall not extend beyond the 31st March 1931. This declaration concerns also the Reichspost and the German Railway Company.

3. Moreover, the above-mentioned declaration of the German Government lapses in the following cases:

(*a*) Immediately upon the effective accomplishment of mobilisation operations for the amount mentioned above;

(*b*) Two months after the Bank for International Settlements has notified, in accordance with the provisions of Article 143 of the Annexes to the Plan, that it appears to be practicable to proceed with the issue of the amount suggested above, or of an issue completing the amount if owing to the Creditor Powers this issue has not taken place.

II

6. The German Government reserves to itself the right to participate in the mobilisation issue of an amount of 300 million dollars specified in paragraph 1 above. This participation will take place on the original terms.

7. These operations will be carried out through the Bank for International Settlements. The proceeds and the service of the loan shall be divided between the reparation creditors who have a share in the unconditional part of the annuities and the German Government in the proportion of two-thirds for the former and one-third for the latter.

8. The charges for such loans shall be covered in the above proportions by a deduction from reparation payments and by a payment by the Reich to the Bank for International Settlements. In the case of each of these loans, the sums provided by this deduction and this payment shall be merged by the Bank for International Settlements in an account exclusively and solely reserved for the service of this loan.

APPENDIX XIV

THE BANK AND BULGARIAN REPARATIONS

The following are extracts from the "Agreement with Bulgaria" concluded at The Hague in January 1930:

AGREEMENT WITH BULGARIA

(3) The annuities fixed in Article 2 shall constitute an unconditional obligation and the parties signatory to the present agreement waive their right to demand the application of Article 122 of the Treaty of Neuilly. Bulgaria may, however, if the need arises, request the application of the system of postponement of transfer instituted by the Reparation Commission's decision of 23rd July 1926, pursuant to the Financial Scheme approved on 10th June 1926 by the Council of the League of Nations.

These annuities shall enjoy the benefit of the same special securities as are assigned to the annuities of the Schedule of Payments of 21st March 1923, by virtue of the Protocols of 21st March 1923 and 24th September 1928. They shall be represented by a debt certificate, with coupons attached, which shall be handed over by the Bulgarian Government to the Bank for International Settlements acting as trustee for the Creditor Powers.

The first charge established by Article 132 of the Treaty of Neuilly upon all the assets and revenues of Bulgaria for the cost of reparation and other costs referred to in that Article shall cease to have effect. But if the product of the special securities falls below 150 per cent of the sums necessary for the service of the annuity, the Bulgarian Government undertakes at the request of the Bank for International Settlements, to assign to reparations additional securities which shall be considered acceptable by the said Bank and shall at least restore the said percentage, and to promulgate any laws necessary for this purpose.

(4) The National Bank of Bulgaria shall retain its present functions and obligations in regard to the payment of reparations arising out of the Regulations of 7th July 1923 regarding the application of the Protocol of 21st March 1923, and shall comply with those Regulations in regard to the collection of the proceeds from the securities, the constitution in national currency of the annuity funds and their conversion into foreign currencies.

(5) The rights and powers conferred on the Reparation Commission and on the Interallied Commission in Bulgaria shall, in so far as is necessary, be transferred to the Bank for International Settlements.

Consequently, the relations between the Reparation Commission and the Interallied Commission in Bulgaria, of the one part, and the Bulgarian Government, of the other part, shall terminate as soon as possible. The conditions and the date of this transfer shall be determined by a Committee consisting of two representatives of the Bulgarian Government, of four representatives of the Reparation Commission, or of the Interallied Commission in Bulgaria (one of whom shall be the common delegate on the Reparation Commission or a representative appointed by him), and, if possible, of two representatives of the Bank for International Settlements.

. . . .

(13) Should the Bank for International Settlements not accept the whole of the functions attributed to it by the present Agreement, the appointment of some other trustee to be substituted so far as necessary for the Bank will form part of the task of the Committee constituted under Article 5.

APPENDIX XV

THE BANK AND HUNGARIAN REPARATIONS

The following are extracts from Annex IV. to the "Agreement Relating to Hungarian Obligations under the Treaty" concluded at The Hague in January 1930:

ANNEX IV

AGREEMENT BETWEEN THE HUNGARIAN GOVERNMENT AND THE CREDITOR GOVERNMENTS

3. The payments due up to the 1st January 1944 shall be subject to the conditions laid down in the texts actually in force and particularly in the decision No. 2797 of the Reparation Commission. However, they shall be paid to the Bank for International Settlements for the account of the Creditor States.

4. The payments due after 1944 constitute an unconditional obligation, that is to say, without any rights of suspension whatsoever. They shall be made in gold or in currency equivalent to gold in equal half-yearly periods on the 1st January and 1st July of each year, the first payment falling due on the 1st January 1944. Like the preceding payments they shall be made to the Bank for International Settlements for the account of the Creditor States.

. . . .

7. The Hungarian Government shall transmit to the Bank for International Settlements in its capacity of Trustee for the Creditor Powers certificates representing the annuities specified

under 1, which certificates in their text should carry out the provisions of Articles 3 and 5.

.   .   .   .

10. The relations between the Reparation Commission and Hungary shall be terminated as soon as possible.

The rights and powers conferred on the Reparation Commission shall be transferred as far as necessary to the Bank for International Settlements. The procedure and date for this transfer shall be laid down by a Committee formed of two representatives of the Hungarian Government, by four representatives of the Reparation Commission, to include the Common Delegate on the Reparation Commission, or a representative nominated by him, and by a representative of the Bank for International Settlements.

APPENDIX XVI

THE BANK AND CZECHOSLOVAKIAN
LIBERATION DEBT

The following are extracts from the "Agreement with Czechoslovakia" concluded at The Hague in January 1930:

AGREEMENT WITH CZECHOSLOVAKIA

Article 2

The instalments shall be paid by the Czechoslovak Government to the Bank for International Settlements, for the account of the Creditor Governments, in pounds sterling, at the average rate of exchange for the three days preceding the date of payment.

The Bank shall transfer the sums encashed to the account of each of the Creditor Governments, in accordance with the rules for distribution fixed by the Arrangement between the Creditor Powers (Austria, Hungary, Bulgaria, Liberation Debt) concluded at The Hague Conference, 1930, and with any special arrangement between two or more of these Governments concerning their respective shares, as fixed by the said Agreement which shall have been notified to the Bank by the Creditor Governments concerned.

.   .   .   .

Should the Bank for International Settlements not accept in its entirety the mandate with which it is entrusted by the present agreement, it shall be the duty of the Committee formed as mentioned above to formulate the amendments necessary to obtain its complete adoption, and failing that to choose a Trustee as far as this may concern the Bank.

Printed in Great Britain by R. & R. CLARK, LIMITED, *Edinburgh.*